*For Morton —
With great appreciation
for your significant
contribution to my dream
pilgrimage
Lois Hendricks*

DISCOVERING MY BIBLICAL DREAM HERITAGE

Lois Lindsey Hendricks

RESOURCE PUBLICATIONS, INC. • San Jose, California

Editorial director: Kenneth Guentert
Production editor: Elizabeth J. Asborno
Cover design and production: Andrew Wong
Back cover photo: Don Arnold & Son Studio
Editorial assistant: Linda D'Angelo

© 1989 Resource Publications, Inc. All rights reserved. For reprint permission, write

Reprint Department
Resource Publications, Inc.
160 E. Virginia St., # 290
San Jose, CA 95112

Library of Congress Cataloging in Publication Data

Hendricks, Lois Lindsey, 1926-
  Discovering my Biblical dream heritage.

  1. Dreams in the Bible. 2. Visions in the Bible.
3. Dreams—History. 4. Visions—History. I. Title
BF1099.B5H46 1989 220.8'15463 89-10250
ISBN 0-89390-144-X

5 4 3 2 1
93 92 91 90 89

Grateful acknowledgment is made to the following for permission to reprint:

From THE NEW ENGLISH BIBLE WITH APOCRYPHA. © 1961, 1970 The Delegates of the Oxford University Press and the Syndics of the Cambridge University Press. Reprinted with permission.

Scripture taken from the HOLY BIBLE, NEW INTERNATIONAL VERSION. Copyright © 1973, 1978, 1984 International Bible Society. Used by permission of Zondervan Bible Publishers.

From the *Williams New Testament, The New Testament in the Language of the People,* by Charles B. Williams. © Copyright 1937, 1966, 1986 Holman Bible Publishers. Used by permission.

From *Disciples Study Bible.* © Copyright 1988 Holman Bible Publishers. All rights reserved. International copyright secured. Used by permission.

"The Martyrdom of Perpetua" originally appeared in A LOST TRADITION, by Patricia Wilson-Kastner, et. al., copyright 1982 by University Press of America.

Contents

Foreword by Gayle Delaney vi
Preface ix
Introduction 1

Part One
Dreams and Visions in the Hebrew Bible

A Dream Helps Found a Nation and a Religion 9
A Dream Protects the Matriarch of the Hebrew Nation . . . 13
Jacob: Dreams Preserve the Covenant People 17
Joseph and Daniel: Two Interpreters of Others' Dreams . . 23
A Criminal's Vision and Conversation with God 39
A Diviner's Dream Blesses God's People 43
A Midianite Soldier's Dream Predicts Victory for Israel . . . 45
A Child's Scary Dream Has Far-reaching Implications . . . 47
A Prophet Dreams a Message for the King 49
A Dream as a Source of Wisdom 55
A Vision of God's Holiness 59
Summary of Dreams and Visions in the Hebrew Bible 63

Part Two
Dreams and Visions in the Apocrypha

Dreams in the Intertestamental Period 69
A Persian Queen's Cousin Dreams and Saves God's People 73
Summary of Dreams and Visions in the Apocrypha 77

Part Three
Dreams and Visions in the New Testament

Historical Background of New Testament Dreams 81
A Foster Father-to-be Dreams 83
Jesus and Dreams 87
The Apostles and Dreams 91
Night Visions Lead to the Expansion of Christianity 95
Visions of an Exiled Early Christian Leader 101
Summary of Dreams and Visions in the New Testament . 111

Part Four
Dreams and Visions among Post-Biblical Jews

Dreams and Later Judaism 115
Visitational Dreams among Moroccan Jews in Israel 123

Part Five
Dreams and Visions in the Early Church

Dreams Prepare Early Christian Protesters
  for Martyrdom 127
Dreams among Early Church Leaders 139

Part Six
Dreams Today

Our Ordinary Dreams and the Bible 149
Our Extraordinary Dreams 169

Conclusion 189
Notes 199
Appendix: A Guide to Biblical Dreams and Visions 211
Bibliography 237
Index 241

Foreword

Lois Hendricks has taken a courageous and marvelous journey. She has sought out the significance of dreams in the Biblical tradition and in her own life's path. In the pages that follow, Lois takes us on this voyage with her and shows us how the study of dreams in the Bible and in one's nightly life can enrich both our appreciation for the religious and the daily problem solving functions of dreaming.

I first worked with Lois when she was a member of an intensive, ongoing dream study group dedicated to teaching members how to interpret their own dreams. I was struck, as I think you will be, by her forthrightness and courage in facing the material her dreams offered her. Whenever she took on the role of the interviewer who would help the dreamer interpret his or her own dream, I was struck as well by her gently modesty, so rare among dream experts, which allowed her to skillfully draw out of the dreamer the meaning of the dream rather than impose an interpretation from outside the dreamer. Lois' understanding that dreams are often very personal metaphors and parables about the dreamer's emotional, spiritual, physical, and creative life has made her a careful dreamworker who respects both the beauty and the specialness of each dream and of each dreamer.

In 1983 the Association for the Study of Dreams was established as an organization dedicated to encouraging the interdisciplinary study of dreams with membership open to

Foreword

practitioners, scholars, and researchers, as well as to the general public. The first months of most organizations shake out the talkers who are not doers. ASD was no different, and I found myself stranded with very few workers to put on our first international conference in San Francisco in 1984. Lois was one of the heroes who came out of the woodwork to take on the job of secretary of the association. She also acted as our membership chairperson and willing volunteer for whatever needed doing. Most importantly, Lois, remained throughout our hectic early days an invaluably dependable, supportive, generous, and cheerful team member. During the closing ceremonies of our first conference, as I looked with delight and relief at the many wonderful people we had gathered together, I burst into tears when I saw Lois. She had been so loving and helpful, and now she had to move away from San Francisco! I would miss her terribly.

What a pleasure it is, six years later, to read and introduce to you this wonderful book! In exploring the biblical dream tradition, Lois is never pedantic but always straightforward and personal in her approach. In suggesting how you might begin to study and understand your own nightly dreams, she clearly describes various biblical and modern methods of interpretation that can open your eyes and your heart to the vast resources of insight available in dreams. Lois bravely shows us a few of her own dreams and the ways she came to understand them and herself better. She reveals how her dreams helped to enrich her spiritual as well as her personal life.

Lois is a skilled dreamworker who has lectured and taught on the subject in Asia, the United States, and Europe. Her sensitivity to the uniqueness of each person's dream experience and to the often idiosyncratic nature of a given dream image makes this book both a good introduction and a sophisticated guide to interpretation based on the private experience and common sense of the dreamer, *not* on any prefabricated, rigid, superstitious dream formulae.

Discovering My Biblical Dream Heritage is an important addition to the literature on dreams that for so long has been

Foreword

lacking in serious but readable and practical explorations of the role of dreams in biblical writings. In the pages that follow, Lois Hendricks will show you the many spiritual and personal benefits of reflecting on that nightly part of our lives that we know as dreaming.

Gayle M. V. Delaney, Ph.D
Founding President of the Association for the Study of
  Dreams
Author of *Living Your Dreams* (Harper & Row, 1988 revised
  edition)

Preface

The primary purpose of this book is to learn how ancient dreamers valued dreams, gain an appreciation for the place dreams have played in our Jewish and Christian traditions, and discover from them how we might honor our everyday dreams and benefit from them.

My personal dream roots go back to when I was ten years old. My three-and-a-half-year-old sister had died and been buried on Easter Sunday. She was buried in a light blue with pink trim taffeta dress with a tiered gathered skirt and puffed sleeves, and she had the white blossom of an Easter lily in her hand. Not long afterward, I saw her in a dream. She was wearing the same dress and carrying the Easter lily blossom; she was walking down the road toward our home on a beautiful sunny morning. She was well and smiling, and I woke up feeling good. I've cherished this dream to myself all these years because I felt as a child that the specialness of it would be diminished by telling it. Perhaps others needed the message it gave me: that she was well and no longer in pain, and that life continues after this one. I had only heard dreams discussed with amusement and then forgotten. Then, too, talking about her death was not done in our family just then--the wound was too raw to handle.

The only other dream I recall while I was growing up was a flying and falling dream. In it I am flying a little Donald Duck-looking airplane. At the time I had never seen an airplane

Preface

close or been in one, so it may have been an image I picked up from a Donald Duck cartoon. The airplane fell apart in the sky, and there I was tumbling about in the sky with pieces, bolts, and screws of the airplane. It was very humorous really, and I recall no fear attached to it. There was a curious sensation of being both in the dream and watching it at the same time.

Subsequent dreams later in life and other life events led me to look at my dreams and think about dreams in general. From childhood I was puzzled that the Bible mentioned dreams, but not much was made of the place dreams had in total biblical narrative. Except for Jacob's dream of angels going up and down a ladder to heaven and his son Joseph' dreams, which were treated almost as entertaining children's stories, it was as though there were no dreams, or that dreams weren't used by God anymore so they weren't important.

Recognizing that dreaming is an experience we all have in common with one another and with all people who have lived, I felt drawn to investigating the use of dreams historically and especially religiously. I discovered that the major world religions, including Judaism and Christianity, had their beginnings in dreams. Being of the Christian community and a descendant of one who was of the Jewish community, I was eager to learn more about their dream traditions. At the time I could scarcely find a mention of dreams in theological and biblical commentaries. I found nothing until my theologian husband, who enjoys browsing bookstores, found a book he thought I might like, entitled, *God, Dreams, and Revelation* by Morton T. Kelsey (Minneapolis, MN: Augsburg Publishing House, 1974). It has been an invaluable resource, helping me to learn about my religious dream heritage.

Until then, and afterward as well, I simply examined the dream passages in the Bible in its various versions and translations. My method was to read the narratives from the viewpoint of the dreamer. Interacting with the dreamers and their dreams in the Bible helped the biblical material become more meaningful to me; it helped me see my own dreaming as an important factor in understanding the realities of my life.

Preface

I also took note of the amount of material concerning dreams. I could not help but feel that denying dreams as the source of material was like leaving out part of the Bible and took away some of the greatness and mystery of God. Allowing dreams their own place in the biblical story served to enhance the Bible for me.

Interestingly enough, my first sources for learning about dream traditions as well as about dreams in general and in my own life were psychologists and psychiatrists, not Bible teachers or theologians (with the exception of one pastoral care minister of the Episcopal Church). By reading their books and attending workshops, I became acquainted with persons who worked with dreams and the various approaches used to understand dreams. But I usually had to arrive at the spiritual insights into my dreams in my own way. Seeing how the dreamers in the Bible did it was my only outside guidance in this area. My first consistent help was several weeks with Chuck Holland, a counselor in Ft. Worth, Texas (where I lived at the time) and a member of the church I attended. That was just before I moved to San Francisco, California, and while it was very helpful, I still didn't feel very secure on my own. After I moved to San Francisco, I met Dr. Gayle Delaney, who was autographing her book in my neighborhood bookstore. From this meeting came the opportunities to work with my own dreams, with the dreams of others, and to serve with her as secretary of the Association for the Study of Dreams, of which she was president. She continues to be a professional consultant to me in my work and in my study of dreams, as well as a dear friend.

I continue my work with dreams in various ways. Primarily, I lead small group conferences, both for international student retreats and in countries where I've traveled. I've done this type of dreamwork for several years. I have found that dreams cut through all political, cultural, and religious barriers. To be accepted, all I usually have to do is ask people how they value dreams in their personal lives and how their culture or religion values dreams, and then I listen. To speak and share and listen

Preface

to one another's dreams and ponder them gives us a feeling of connectedness with each other and with all humanity and touches on something so deep I can only describe it as having a mystical, spiritual quality. It is not difficult to see how, from the earliest times of recorded history, humankind's deepest thoughts have been reflected in and influenced by dreams.

It is from these experiences and the interest of others that this book is being written. It is the book I wished I could have found when I first became interested in the spiritual and religious aspects of dreaming.

Introduction

ANCIENT NEAR EASTERN DREAM PRACTICES

The roots of Jewish-Christian dream traditions go back to the ancient people of the cultures from which they originated.[1] The ancient peoples of Mesopotamia and Egypt, including the ancient Hebrews, respected their dreams and recorded them even before the Greeks did. The cultures of the Ancient Near East believed that there was a spiritual reality that broke in upon the individual's physical reality. They all believed their gods communicated with them through dreams. They often practiced seeking dreams in sacred places and sanctuaries.[2]

The ancient Hebrews followed the same practice of recording their dreams as other Ancient Near Eastern people. However, we find emphasis placed on a more careful interpretation of dreams by the Hebrews, as evidenced in the Hebrew Bible in Deuteronomy and the prophets. Rather than the dream, what God was saying and doing in their lives is emphasized. The message of the dream was considered in the context of their total lives.

Ancient Near Eastern people classified dreams in the following three categories:

Introduction

1. dreams that reveal the deity;
2. dreams that reflect the mental, spiritual, and bodily health of the dreamer;
3. dreams that predict.

Ordinary dreams fell in the second category and were not usually recorded. These will be discussed in another section. Of the recorded dreams in the first and third categories we have very little for the psychiatrist or psychologist to work with, since they reflect little of the psychological aspirations and conflicts of the individual dreamer, and not enough is known of the dreamer's personal background.[3]

These early people followed a rather stylized form of reporting their dreams. A dream report consists of a **frame** and its **content**. The frame describes "the setting of the dream, informs us who is experiencing it and when, where, and under what circumstances...The first part of the frame stresses the fact that the person who is to experience the dream has gone to bed and is deeply asleep." In addition to telling us about the dreamer, the locality, and other circumstances, "the frame describes the end of the dream and often the reaction of the dreamer as well as the fulfillment of the prediction or promise contained in the dream. The content of the dream is embedded within the frame."

Dreams considered a revelation of the deity were of two kinds: Those requiring no interpretation and therefore simply called **message dreams**, and those not expressed in clear words and called **symbolic dreams**.

These symbolic dreams contain a baffling variety of strange images, unusual activities, and humans whose impressive performances disturb yet interest the dreamer. These dreams required interpretation because the message was difficult for the dreamer to understand. However, in some symbolic dreams interpretation did not seem necessary. Joseph's foretelling his future supremacy over his family (Genesis 37:5f.) is a biblical example of a self-explanatory dream. (This dream will be discussed later.) There is another reason why symbolic dreams require the art of the interpreter. The interpreter must be able to help the dreamer establish "whether the dream is to be ignored as devoid of meaning or whether it is to be recognized as bearing on himself, his family or his country."[4]

In the Hebrew Bible, symbolic dreams that require interpretation are more commonly reported by the non-Hebrew, as with Pharaoh and Nebuchadnezzar in the stories of Joseph and Daniel. The Lord sends interpreters to make his message understandable. When divine message is revealed to God's people in dreams, the Lord speaks in simple message dreams and not in "dark speeches" (Numbers 12:8), and He gives understanding at the same time.[5] "...Clever interpretation of dreams was greatly admired" throughout the ancient Near East. This is important to remember in the Bible stories of Joseph and Daniel. "Outside the peculiar religious climate of Israel (Palestine), the recognition as well as the interpretation of the symbolic dream is considered as depending on the intelligence of the dreaming person." Determining whether a non-rational dream was meaningful was just as important as interpreting the dream content into understandable terms. Both abilities as well as the dream itself were traced to the same source: God, "the revealer of mysteries" (Daniel 2:9).

The best collection of recorded dreams from the Ancient Near East is found in the Bible. In those days, dreams were related with equal importance to the events of the day; the people's dreams and their responses to these dreams helped to shape their history and continue to do so today. In this way, the religious dream tradition of the West continues.

The dream stories in the Bible are to me much like "to be continued" stories of God's working in the lives of all humankind, as well as personal episodes in the lives of the dreamers. I am intrigued by the thought that dreams may be continued from one age to another through different individuals.

Introduction

DREAMS IN THE HEBREW BIBLE

Dreams in the Hebrew Bible begin with Abraham. But before we look at these early dreams, we should look at the background from which these dreamers and their dreams came, just as we would look at the backgrounds and settings from which our own dreams came in order to understand them better.

The history of the Jewish people begins with Abraham in Ur of Chaldees (ancient Babylonia). Ur was a prosperous city on the banks of the River Euphrates. The tools and weapons of these people were made of copper and bronze. Iron was rare, for only a few people like the Hittites knew the secret of smelting. The people of Ur were idol worshipers. They worshiped the moon god and many lesser gods. These gods were demanding, cruel, and easily angered. They could be bribed and manipulated.

Abraham and his people along with other tribes lived on the edges of the ancient cities. They were tent-dwelling shepherds and camel owners whose lives centered around their families or tribes rather than a city or a nation. These wandering people followed water and grazing lands for their flocks. The path most followed was northward and down into Canaan (Palestine) and on to Egypt, linking together the two centers of civilization, Egypt and Mesopotamia. Abraham's father led one of these bands of wanderers to a town called Haran in Mesopotamia (now Iraq).

In Haran Abraham rejected his father's gods and set off with his own flocks to lead an independent life. When Abraham's father died, Abraham assumed the leadership of his tribe. This is when Abraham understood the Lord to be instructing him to leave and go to a land that he would be shown (Gen. 12:1), in which he would become a blessing with a great promise. The promise was "I will make of thee a great nation...and in thee shall all families of the earth be blessed" (Gen. 12:2-3). This blessing marks the historical beginning of a special relationship

Introduction

between God and Abraham, which would later result in a nation devoted to the Lord as one God. Dreams were a significant part of this development.

Abraham and his people left Haran and went into Canaan (Palestine). There he found walled cities inhabited by sensitive people using superior weapons. These people worshiped Baal. Here Abraham experienced the Lord saying to him, "This is the land I will give to your descendants." Abraham responded by building his first altar. His people were still herdsmen living in tents and driving their flocks from well to well and searching for grazing land, so they made no attempt to settle down at this time. They journeyed on until a famine made it necessary for them to return to Canaan, where Abraham lived out his life. The first piece of land owned by the Hebrew tribe in Canaan was purchased from a Hittite tribesman for a burial site.

Even before Abraham began to have a well-developed notion of the one God people believed they could know the spiritual world through dreams and visions. Non-technological people with primitive religions today still believe the spiritual dimensions of reality speak to people through dreams, as do most people except those in our Western culture.

The Ancient Near Eastern people, including the Hebrews, did not make a clear distinction between dreams and visions. In this writing I use mostly those experiences designated as dreams, also called visions by night or visions in the sleep. This is because dreams are a more common experience to us, thus making our discussion of them more manageable. This does not mean I consider less important visions and spiritual experience such as talking with God, seeing angels, and related manifestations.

Biblical dreams are usually considered special dreams from God to reveal his nature and grace to his creation. Even so, they include the same elements as our everyday dreams. By looking at them, we may understand our dreams better. We can learn who we really are and how God works in our everyday lives; we

Introduction

can find direction and guidance and healing in them; and we can find ways to relate our dreams to God and use our dreams to enrich our relationship to God.

First, I let the dreamer relate the dream. Then I review briefly the life of the dreamer and observe how the dreamer responded to the dream. Finally, I will relate all of this to our present-day dreams. Sometimes, with the help of various translations, I paraphrase the dream, putting it into first person so as to let the dreamer speak more directly to the reader; however, the Scripture reference is given for those who desire to read it directly from their own Bibles.

Part One
Dreams and Visions in the Hebrew Bible

Chapter 1

A Dream Helps Found a Nation and a Religion

> As the sun was setting, "I fell asleep and a great terror came over me, I heard the Lord say to me that his promise to me and my descendants to make of us a great nation would be fulfilled, but there would be a long delay. The delay would be caused by the wickedness of the enemies. The sun went down and it was dusk, and I saw a smoking firepot and a flaming torch passing between the divided pieces."

Dreamer: Abraham
Source: Genesis 15:7-21, paraphrase of Genesis 15:12

Abraham is the ancestor of the Israelite people. His name was Abram, meaning *high father*, but God later changed it to Abraham, meaning *father of many nations* (Genesis 17). This dream prepared Abraham for his destiny. What he heard reassured him that the promise would be fulfilled, but not before a long delay; thus he prepared for the fulfillment of this promise to be slow in coming.

In the last part of the dream he sees images and symbols. These dream images, which are so strange to us, probably did not seem strange to Abraham. They came out of the everyday experiences

Part One: Dreams and Visions in the Hebrew Bible

of his life. "The divided pieces" referred to the ritual animal sacrifice Abraham had just made previous to his falling asleep. This ceremony had been prescribed by God in conversation with Abraham to ensure him that he would gain possession of the promised land. This ancient ceremony was used for making contracts between equal parties. Two parties sacrificed an animal by cutting it in half and laying the pieces down opposite each other. Then both parties walked between the pieces of the carcass, demonstrating their willingness to be bound by the agreement or suffer the same treatment.

The "smoking pot" was used for cooking. Abraham understood it to symbolize himself and humankind. Fire was a symbol of deity, thus the "flaming torch" symbolized the presence of God.

While these images were from Abraham's everyday life, they were put together in a surprising way. Abraham saw this as a covenant between God and himself, and as a message from God: "To your descendants I give this land..." (Genesis 15:18).

This is an example of how a dream prepares us for unexpected circumstances and gives us assurance. Reverend Trautman, in *The Bible Today* (October 1975), says this dream led Abraham to leave "the world of his ancestors and set off into the unknown, into uncertainty, risk all that he had, sacrifice the present for the sake of what was to come; he let go of what was safe and calculable for the sake of what was unknown."

We may not be called to be an ancestor of a new nation in order to bless all people, but part of life is a constant letting go of the safe and known and facing the unknown. Our personal dreams can be a resource to prepare and reassure us in our own times of crises and transition.

Changing jobs and moving to a new geographic area are two of these transition experiences. I have geographically relocated twice since 1950. Dreams have accompanied both moves. One involved a career move to San Francisco from Texas. I had the dream even before my husband was invited to consider this new position, and it occurred amid dreams dealing with other issues;

A Dream Helps Found a Nation and a Religion

therefore, it was very puzzling. Within a week we were considering this move. It was then that I understood this dream was related to this event in my life.

In the dream, I am taking things out of an old cornerstone from a building being torn down. Among them are a huge round of cheese and a favorite plaid cotton dress, in shady greens and pinks on white, which I had worn when we were first married. Next I am faced with decisions such as what will go into packing a new cornerstone.

Events previous to considering this move had no doubt put the possibility into my subconscious. At the time of this dream, my husband, Bill, was in the San Francisco Bay Area on a speaking engagement. He would be seeing a former colleague and friend who had recently taken a position as president of Golden Gate Theological Seminary in Mill Valley, California. Two years before, Bill had seriously considered taking a teaching position there. I had thought so strongly that he would accept the position that I had investigated job possibilities for myself. Bill did not take the position; however the experience led him to examine what his future would include in the twenty years before retirement. Now that a friend was there and he was visiting in the area, the possibility of his being asked to reconsider crossed my mind. I believe my subconscious put all this together, resulting in my dream and preparing my mind for what happened soon after. Indeed, my husband was offered the position with an expanded job description, and he accepted it. The dream had suggested that the stuff that had made up my life was passing, leaving behind its mementos, and now it was time to make decisions about the next phase of my life. Later I realized that dreams frequently accompanied moves to new geographical locations in biblical narratives.

I have learned from international students that this is not an unusual experience for them either. The first to share this with me was an African student from Sudan, who said to me, "I used to have dreams of coming to the U.S. for college and here I am at the Ohio State University."

Chapter 2

A Dream Protects the Matriarch of the Hebrew Nation

> God came to me in a dream one night and said to me, "You are as good as dead because of the woman you have taken; she is a married woman." Now I had not gone near her, so I said, "Lord, will you destroy an innocent nation? Did Abraham not say to me, 'She is my sister,' and didn't she also say, 'He is my brother'? I have done this with a clear conscience and clean hands." Then God said to me in the dream, "Yes, I know you did this with a clear conscience, and so I have kept you from sinning against me. This is why I did not let you touch her. Now return the man's wife, for he is a prophet, and he will pray for you and you will live. But if you do not return her, you may be sure that you and all yours will die.'"

Dreamer: King Abimelech
Source: Genesis 20: 3-7, paraphrased in first person

Abimelech was king of the ancient city Gerar by the Nile River in Egypt. Abraham and his wife, Sarah, had gone there in search of food in time of famine in Canaan. Abraham became afraid that he might be killed and his wife

Part One: Dreams and Visions in the Hebrew Bible

Sarah taken, so he and Sarah pretended to be brother and sister. King Abimelech did send for her and she went to live in his court. She may really have been Abraham's half-sister, because in those days marriage to a half-sister was permitted. Other ancient writings mention that one's wife could be legally adopted as a sister (The Nuzi Text). However, what Abraham and Sarah did was considered a lie by both Abimelech and God.

Sarah's identity was revealed to King Abimelech in what is today called a **clairvoyant** dream. A clairvoyant dream presents the dreamer with information the dreamer didn't know and couldn't possibly have known. Abimelech may have sensed intuitively that something wasn't right with this situation, but the dream brought the issue to his conscious attention. This dream appears to be a warning. On another level it is a means of resolving a problem between Abimelech and Abraham.

We won't likely be protected as Sarah was by a dream in order to save a nation about to be born. We might not even have a dream as King Abimelech did that will reveal information that couldn't be known otherwise. But we probably will have a dream that helps to define and resolve a problem.

By means of this dream, Sarah was protected so God's promise to Abraham could be realized. It also taught a gentle lesson to Abraham and Sarah that God would keep his promise, even when they fell short, and would take care of them without their lying and manipulation. "God's grace does not depend upon human worthiness...." King Abimelech was not a believer in the one God of the Hebrews, but people of all religions valued dreams and looked to them to find meaning for their lives. The history of the Hebrew people was sometimes shaped and directed by dreams of the non-Hebrew people as well as their own.

Abraham had two sons, Ishmael and Isaac, born in Canaan. Ishmael became the founder of the Arab nations. Isaac became the ancestor of the Israelite people. Isaac is not recorded as being a dreamer, but the Lord renews his covenant with him

A Dream Protects the Matriarch of the Hebrew Nation

and reassures him through special appearances, and he became father of Jacob, the third great patriarch who is a great dreamer.

Chapter 3

Jacob: Dreams Preserve the Covenant People

> I had a dream in which I saw a stairway (ladder) resting on the earth, with its top reaching to heaven, and the angels of God ascending and descending on it. There above it stood the Lord, and he said: "I am the Lord, the God of your father Abraham and God of Isaac. I will give you and your descendants the land on which you are lying. Your descendants will be like the dust of the earth, and you will spread out to the west and to the east, to the north and to the south. All people on earth will be blessed through you and your offspring. I am with you and will watch over you wherever you go, and I will bring you back to this land. I will not leave you until I have done what I have promised you."

Dreamer: Jacob
Source: Genesis 28:11-15, from Genesis 27:41-28:28, paraphrased in first person

Jacob, Abraham's grandson, was running away from his home in Beersheba when he had this dream. He had cheated his brother and was on his way to Haran to live

Part One: Dreams and Visions in the Hebrew Bible

with his Uncle Laban. His brother had threatened to kill him. He had never been away from home before, and he missed the warmth and comfort of the family campsite. One night he chose a stone for a pillow and wrapped up in his cloak, and he fell asleep and had this beautiful dream of God's messengers going up and down a ladder on God's business. Suddenly God seemed very close. Then Jacob heard God speaking to him. He was repeating the promise of safety that he had previously made to Abraham. When Jacob awoke he was so impressed he felt he had chanced upon the place of God's abode. He immediately responded with conversation. Quite often we find Bible dreams accompanied with conversation or dialogue between the dreamer and God. It's almost as though the images and symbols are meant to get attention and invite conversation. All that Jacob had seen and heard certainly got his attention, and he said, "Lord God, if you are really here, then help me to make a new start in life. I'm a young man, alone in the world, and without a home or a job. If you will help me now, then I shall certainly worship you" (Fount Children's Bible, trans. William Collins and Co., Ltd., London: Fount Paperbacks, 1981).

He took the stone he had slept on and made an altar. He named the place Bethel, or house of God, and he made a commitment to give a tithe to God.

Jacob does not translate the imagery of the ladder and angels into a message as we so often do. He responded to the dream experience as a whole. To him it meant that God was in this place with a runaway, and he was inspired by the experience to take immediate action. He accepted the covenant relationship and chose to continue the responsibility to be a parent of a people that would bless all people.

When we stop to think about how the simple reading of Jacob's dream experience affects people even to this day, it is not surprising that he responded to it so fully and so strongly. It is probably the best-known biblical dream; it comes to mind first when asked to recall a dream from the Bible. Laurens van

Jacob: Dreams Preserve the Covenant People

der Post, in his book *Jung and the Story of Our Time,* calls it the greatest dream ever dreamt and recalls his grandfather reading it to him from the family Bible when he was a child. He says all he has to do even now is close out the electric-lit day to see within the darkness a ladder pitched on the stony ground of a great wasteland, reaching high to a star-packed heaven, with the urgent traffic of angels phosphorescent upon it. To Laurens van der Post, the image of the ladder positioned between heaven and earth conveys the meaning that the Source of dreams will be in communion with humankind forever; that Jacob's state and the great wasteland through which he is fleeing in fear for his life is the image of all people without help, at the end of their resources from within and without; and that the angels are visualizations of messengers by which the Source and the dreamer can communicate.

Through the dream the creator promised him and those who were to follow after help to the end of their days. The remarkable thing is that Jacob had not even to ask for it. He was not even aware of God's presence before this dream. He had thought himself alone and abandoned.

Jacob related to his dream experience in such a way as to promote his growth as a person and as a leader. We can learn much from Jacob and this dream that will help us to use our dreams wisely.

- We can consider the possibility of God's inviting us to converse with him.

- We can, with some dreams, respond to the total experience.

- We can respond by taking action that will promote growth.

The personal story of Henry Reed[1] is a contemporary illustration of responding to a dream experience as a whole. As a very young man he, too, was troubled, and in the seventh year of alcoholism was searching for a way out. One night, feeling totally helpless, lonely, and sorry for himself as he con-

Part One: Dreams and Visions in the Hebrew Bible

templated his future as an "unredeemable, drunken bum," he drank himself to sleep. A few hours later, he woke up sobbing uncontrollably. His crying was a carry-over of this dream:

> I am amidst a crowd of people. We are looking up into the sky. It is night and yet the sun is up and acting strangely. Rays of light shoot out in all directions across the sky. An eerie tension unites the crowd and the sky. Out from the sun flies a glowing object. As it descends from the sky it appears to be a dove. The dove flies overhead, then zooms right down to me and nestles in my chest. I cry aloud, releasing tears of joy and relief, "Somebody loves me!"

Like Jacob, he related to the total emotional impact of the dream without working on the imagery. He responded with action. Feeling he "might be worth saving" after all, he took hope. He began attending Alcoholics Anonymous meetings, psychoanalytic therapy, and took up dream research. Like Jacob, he responded to his experience in such a way as to promote his growth as a person and a leader. Now he works as a counselor and a teacher, focusing on dreams and relating to them as a means of inspiration for his work with the arts and his own water-color painting.

Jacob had gone on to Haran where his Uncle Laban lived. There he met his match, for Laban was a crafty and deceitful fellow. After twenty years the following dream gave Jacob help in returning to the land of his birth. It is found in Genesis 31:10.

> I once had a dream in which I looked up and saw that the male goats mating with the flock were streaked, speckled or spotted. The angel of God said to me in the dream, "Jacob." I answered, "Here I am." And he said, "Look up and see that all the male goats mating with the flock are streaked, speckled, or spotted, for I have seen all that Laban has been doing to you. I am the God of Bethel, where you anointed a pillar and where you made a vow to me. Now leave this land at once and go back to your native land."

Again Jacob saw an image and was spoken to by the God of Bethel, the place where Jacob had dreamed of the angels on the ladder and made his vow to God. He interpreted the image of the mating goats in the context of an agreement he had made

Jacob: Dreams Preserve the Covenant People

with Laban concerning his wages; he interpreted the whole dream as instruction from God to take with him the livestock he had gained in the flock he had been caring for.

Once again Jacob took action. He left with his family and possessions without even saying good-bye. Once more he is fleeing, this time to thwart the cunning plans of Laban, who, while angrily pursuing Jacob, received the following message from God in a dream by night: "Be careful not to say anything to Jacob either good or bad" (Genesis 31:24).

After a search for stolen goods, Laban entered into an agreement with Jacob and returned home.

Jacob maintained to the end of his life the attitude of his ancestors that dreams were expressions of a reality beyond the physical world, which we call spiritual or non-physical. However, Jacob still had difficulty believing the promise made in his first dream of the angels and the ladder that God would be with him wherever he went. In his last recorded dream, found in Genesis 46:2-4, Jacob is comforted and reassured.

> God spoke to me in vision at night saying "Jacob! I am God, the God of your father. Do not be afraid to go down to Egypt, for I will make you a great nation there. I will go down to Egypt with you, and I will surely bring you back again. And Joseph's own hand will close your eyes."

That dreams can provide us with comfort and reassurance until the end of our lives *is* comforting and reassuring.

Chapter Four

Joseph and Daniel: Two Interpreters of Others' Dreams

Joseph and Daniel are the most famous dreamers and dream interpreters of the Bible. Both interpreted symbolic dreams of those in pagan courts and outside the covenant. The patriarchs, prophets, and others of the Hebrew people knew in a direct way the meaning of the images and symbols without translating this pictorial language into the words and ideas we use in our waking life. They may have presented the derived message in the Bible after they had worked on their dreams, or they may have known the meaning without any work at all. In either instance, they understood the meaning for themselves.

There are interesting similarities in the lives of Joseph and Daniel. Both were captives, then slaves in alien countries. Both rose to power in the government of those countries due to their ability to interpret dreams. Clever interpretation of dreams

Part One: Dreams and Visions in the Hebrew Bible

was greatly admired in both Egypt and Babylonia. The two men considered their ability to interpret dreams to be a gift from God.

"The Lord is always represented as sending a 'symbolic' dream in order to demonstrate to the gentile ruler that his servant alone, whom he himself has instructed in vision, etc., is able to 'decode' the message of the Lord.

"The pious interpreter then puts to shame the gentile experts who dare to attempt to interpret a 'symbolic' dream sent by the Lord. Here, the 'magicians' and 'wise men' of Egypt fail exactly as the magicians, astrologers and sorcerers and Chaldeans of Nebuchadnezzar."[2]

JOSEPH

Joseph was the eleventh and favorite of Jacob's sons. They all lived in the land of Canaan, which had been promised to Joseph's great-great-grandfather, Abraham. They lived a semi-nomadic life as peasants and shepherds, raising small fields of grain near their main camp. Joseph shared the duties of caring for the sheep and harvesting wheat and barley. There was much sibling rivalry between the brothers, who would not say a kind word to Joseph. To make matters worse, Jacob gave Joseph a beautiful coat with long sleeves when Joseph was seventeen. A coat with long sleeves was not worn by peasants and herdsmen because they would be in the way while they were working. The beautiful coat with long sleeves indicated Joseph was intended for a better occupation.[3] Joseph's brothers took this to mean that they weren't considered as good as Joseph, and so they were jealous. As if that were not enough, Joseph did a foolish thing. He told the following dreams; the first he told to his brothers while in the fields harvesting grain, and the second he told to his father and brothers.

Joseph and Daniel: Two Interpreters of Others' Dreams

> Listen to this dream I had: We were binding sheaves of grain out in the field when suddenly my sheaf rose and stood upright, while your sheaves gathered around mine and bowed down to it (Genesis 37:5-7 paraphrased in first person).
>
> Listen, I had another dream, and this time the sun and moon and eleven stars were bowing down to me (Genesis 37:9 paraphrased in first person).

These two dreams of Joseph's are what we now refer to as **recurring** dreams or **repetitive** dreams. While the imagery and symbolism is not the same, they both deal with the same issue. These are examples of symbolic dreams in the Bible, but unlike most symbolic dreams, they are self-explanatory and require no interpretation. "It is evident to Joseph as well as his brothers who the bundles of grain and the stars and sun and moon stand for...." They understood these images to mean that Joseph considered himself superior to them. Not only did they take them to represent the way things were at the moment, they also must have seen a predictive quality in them. Especially does the second one seem to foretell his future supremacy over his family (Genesis 37:5f., and 9f.). Even his father rebuked him. Perhaps he thought the dreams reflected Joseph's attitude at that moment, and he feared the trouble it was causing in the family, or maybe he was just tired of the squabbling between the brothers.

At that time, Joseph in his youth had not acquired the wisdom or sensitivity needed to use the dream to promote healing in the area of family relationships, which is the way it may have been used today. Or maybe he had a great desire to get back at his brothers. While usually the sharing of one's dreams can benefit families by helping them understand one another better, there may be times when dreams are better not told, and this may be one of those times. After all, they were really meant for Joseph and not his family. Joseph experienced these as pleasant dreams; they reassured him that things would be different with his brothers some day.

Part One: Dreams and Visions in the Hebrew Bible

Repeating dreams *do* sometimes assure us that all is going to be well. More often, they are trying to tell us something we aren't aware of or need to pay attention to now. They could have been immediately profitable to Joseph by helping him see himself as the cause of conflict with his brothers. However, symbolic dreams were considered predictive in those days, so Joseph may have experienced them as invitations to converse with God, as did his father. In that way he would have been introduced to his destiny and God's larger purpose for his life. As it turned out, his pleasant dream turned into a nightmare.

One day when his brothers were pasturing the sheep some distance from home, Jacob sent Joseph to find out how they were. The very sight of him in his beautiful coat angered them. They seized him and stripped off his coat. Then they threw him into a pit and planned to leave him. A caravan of Ishmaelite merchants headed for Egypt was passing by. Joseph's brothers took this opportunity to make a little money and sold him into slavery. They tore his coat and stained it with goat's blood and took it to their father, who concluded that Joseph had been destroyed by a wild beast. This is exactly what the brothers want him to think.

Potiphar, captain of Pharaoh's guard, bought Joseph, and the boy worked so well that he became overseer of the whole household. Potiphar's wife became angry with Joseph when he refused her "love" and lied about him, causing him to be put in prison. It was while he was in prison that he earned the reputation as an interpreter of dreams. Two other prisoners, chief servants from Pharaoh's household, came to him with their dreams. Joseph's response was, "Do not interpretations belong to God?" It seems he was learning to be more cautious about dreams.

Joseph and Daniel: Two Interpreters of Others' Dreams

Dreams Told to Joseph While He Was in Prison

The following two dreams were told to Joseph. The first was told by Pharaoh's chief cupbearer; the second, by Pharaoh's chief baker.

> In my dream I saw a vine in front of me with three branches. As soon as it budded, it blossomed, and its cluster ripened into grapes. Pharaoh's cup was in my hand, and I took the grapes, squeezed them into Pharaoh's cup and put the cup in his hand (Genesis 40:9-11).

> I too had a dream. On my head were three baskets of bread. In the top basket were all kinds of baked goods for Pharaoh, but the birds were eating them out of the basket on my head (Genesis 40:16-17).

When Joseph heard their dreams, he predicted one would be restored to his position, but the other would be hanged, and his predictions came true. God used this incident to get Joseph introduced to Pharaoh and out of prison. It was two years before this happened, when Pharaoh was troubled by a nightmare-like, recurrent dream. The servant remembered Joseph and told Pharaoh how accurate he had been in interpreting dreams in prison. Joseph was sent for, and Pharaoh told him these dreams.

Pharaoh's Dreams

> In my dream, I was standing on the Nile, when out of the river there came seven cows, sleek, and fat, and they grazed among the reeds. After them seven other cows came up— scrawny and very ugly and lean. I had never seen such ugly cows in all the land of Egypt. And the lean, ugly cows, ate up the seven fat cows that came up first. But even after they ate them, no one could tell that they had done so. I fell asleep again and had a second dream. I saw seven heads of grain full and good growing on a single stalk. After them seven other heads (of grain) sprouted—withered and thin and scorched by the east wind. The thin heads of grain swallowed up the seven good heads (Genesis 41:17-24).

Part One: Dreams and Visions in the Hebrew Bible

Joseph had already told Pharaoh, "I cannot do it [interpret dreams] but God will give Pharaoh the answer he desires" (Genesis 41:16). This was a polite and pious wish interpreters said when they hoped the dreams would give the dreamer a favorable message. Now Joseph said to Pharaoh, "God has shown you in these dreams what he is about to do" (Genesis 41:25b and 28). Joseph told Pharaoh that God gave the dream in two forms because it was an established fact that a severe famine was going to happen. Nothing could be done to prevent it (Genesis 41:21); however, something could be done to prepare for it so that the country would not be ruined (Genesis 41:33-36).

Pharaoh was so impressed that he named Joseph prime minister of Egypt and second most powerful person in Egypt (Genesis 41:39- 40).

When the famine came, the people around Egypt were also victims of it, and Joseph's father and family were without food. News of Egypt's abundance reached them, and Jacob sent his oldest sons to ask for grain. Joseph was distributing the grain and he recognized his brothers when they bowed down before him, but they did not recognize him. Twenty years had passed and he was no longer a youth, and he was dressed in Egyptian clothes. Also, they were not expecting to see him, certainly not in this position.

No doubt when Joseph saw them bowing before him, he remembered his dreams. He could have said, "I told you so. Remember my dreams. They indicated this would happen—that you would bow down to me." But he was wiser now and had learned to use dreams for good instead of in selfish, hurtful ways. Instead he satisfied himself that his brothers had become more caring for their father and baby brother left at home. Then he identified himself. As might be expected, they were afraid, but he told them not to be afraid, that God had turned evil into good. Not only was the family reunited, but Pharaoh gave them fertile land in Goshen on which to live. Joseph had preserved his people, the people of Abraham, Isaac, and Jacob, with whom God had made a covenant to bless both them and all the people of the earth. That Joseph recognized this was evident in his dying words to his brothers, "God will take you up out of this land promised to Abraham, Isaac and Jacob...then you must carry my bones up from this place" (Genesis 50:24-25).

There certainly are givens and unavoidables that limit our choices and influence our destiny. However, we can choose to commit our life to our destiny as we become aware of it, or we can resist it causing ourselves and others much despair.[4] As it was, Joseph learned more of God's loving care and in turn became a caring, loving person to his family and others.

DANIEL

Daniel had a lot to say about dreams and interpreting them. Daniel was taken into captivity when Babylonia took over Jerusalem by force. He and the most promising young men were taken to Babylon to be educated and prepared to serve in the king's palace.

Daniel could understand visions and dreams of all kinds (Daniel 1:17b). His outstanding abilities came to King Nebuchadnezzar's attention, who promoted him to a high position of leadership right away. King Nebuchadnezzar became troubled to know what his dream was. This statement may mean that he could not remember the dream, but more likely it means he did not know what it meant. This caused him sleepless nights, and he demanded that his wise men not only interpret the dream, but also recall the dream or be killed. None could do this.[5]

When Daniel heard about this, he and his companions prayed to God to disclose the secret to them. "Then in a vision by night the secret was revealed and he blessed God" (Daniel 2:19-20). Daniel told the king that there was a God in heaven who revealed mysteries. He told the king that the mystery was revealed to Daniel not because he had greater wisdom than the

Part One: Dreams and Visions in the Hebrew Bible

king, but so that the king could learn the interpretation and understand what was in his mind. Then he proceeded to tell the dream as follows.

> You looked, O king, and there before you stood a large statue—an enormous, dazzling statue, awesome in appearance. The head of the statue was made of pure gold, its chest and arms of silver, its belly and thighs of bronze, its legs of iron, its feet partly of iron and partly of baked clay. While you were watching, a rock was cut out, but not by human hands. It struck the statue on its feet of iron and clay and smashed them. Then the iron, the clay, the bronze, the silver and the gold were broken to pieces at the same time and became like chaff on a threshing floor in the summer. The wind swept them away without leaving a trace. But the rock that struck the statue became a huge mountain and filled the whole earth. This was the dream, and now we will interpret it to the king (Daniel 2:31-36).

Daniel credited God with the interpretation and told what the enormous, dazzling, awesome dream image was all about. He said the first image represented four kingdoms that would reign one after the other: the gold represented King Nebuchadnezzar's kingdom; the silver, bronze, and iron represented the inferior kingdoms that would follow; and clay represented a weakness that would bring ruin to them all.

The second image is that of a rock that was hewn out from a mountain, but not by a human hand. While not so spectacular in appearance, it did an extraordinary thing. It grew until it became a mountain that filled the whole earth.

In the time of those inferior kingdoms, the God of heaven will set up a kingdom that will never be destroyed, nor will it be left to another people. It will crush all those kingdoms and bring them to an end, but it will itself endure forever. This is the meaning of the rock cut of a mountain, but not by human hands—a rock that broke the iron, the bronze, the clay, the silver, and the gold to pieces.

Daniel told Nebuchadnezzar that the great God had shown the king what would take place in the future. He said that the dream was true and that the interpretation was trustworthy (Daniel 2:44- 45.)

Joseph and Daniel: Two Interpreters of Others' Dreams

Daniel believed that God gave proof of his presence and power through dreams to pagan kings as well as to worshipers of God.

The king accepted this interpretation as correct by acknowledging the supremacy of Daniel's God as a God of gods, Lord of Kings, and revealer of secrets. He made Daniel ruler of Babylon and chief of the sages. It may be that Nebuchadnezzar recognized Daniel's skill more than he recognized Daniel's God. As we shall see later in his next dream, he still had trouble giving God credit and took credit himself for what was possible only as God allowed it.

To reveal another's dream on demand and as the result of one's own seeking is an unusually mysterious dream activity. It was just as unusual then, as all the wise men in Babylon said it couldn't be done, even though their inability cost them their lives. It was not unusual to seek dreams for religious and healing purposes, but seeking someone else's dreams did not fall into this category. Seeking a dream is called **incubating** or **inducing** a dream. Dream incubation includes preparing yourself to receive a dream. Certainly we see this element present in Daniel's preparing himself through prayer and even asking his friends to pray. However, this is a one of a kind dream experience.

Perhaps God enabled Daniel to envision Nebuchadnezzar's forgotten dream by means of telepathy or clairvoyance. He himself explained it by saying it was revealed to him by God (Daniel 2:33).

Nebuchadnezzar dreamed again, and it was so terrifying he sent for his wise men and finally for Daniel, whom the king calls by his Babylonian name, Belteshazzar.

> I had a dream that made me afraid. As I was lying in my bed, the images and visions that passed through my mind terrified me. These are the visions I saw while lying in my bed: I looked, and there before me stood a tree in the middle of the land. Its height was enormous. The tree grew large and strong and its top touched the sky; it was visible to the ends of the earth. Its leaves were beautiful, its fruit abundant, and on it was food for all. Under it the beasts of the field

Part One: Dreams and Visions in the Hebrew Bible

> found shelter, and the birds of the air lived in its branches; from it every creature was fed. In the visions I saw while lying in my bed, I looked, and there before me was a messenger, a holy one, coming down from heaven. He called in a loud voice: "Cut down the tree and trim off its branches; strip off its leaves and scatter its fruit. Let the animals flee from under it and the birds from it branches. But let the stump and its roots, bound with iron and bronze, remain in the ground, in the grass of the field. Let him be drenched with the dew of heaven, and let him live with the animals among the plants of the earth. Let his mind be changed from that of a man and let him be given the mind of an animal, till seven times pass by for him. The decision is announced by messengers, the holy ones declare the verdict, so that the living may know that the Most High is sovereign over the kingdoms of men and gives them to anyone he wishes and sets over them the lowliest of men." This is the dream that I, King Nebuchadnezzar, had. Now, Belteshazzar, tell my what it means, for none of the wise men in my kingdom can interpret it for me. But you can, because the spirit of the holy gods is in you (Daniel 4:5, 10-18)

This dream was so frightening that Daniel began his interpretation by saying, "My lord, if only the dreams were for those who hate you." This is the traditional formula that is meant to direct the evil of the prediction upon the enemies of the dreamer and to introduce bad tidings (Daniel 4:19b). Then he continued.

> The great tree that supplies food and shelter for all life is you, you and your kingdom. (This seems to imply that the animals and birds that live in it are the people of his kingdom.) Your influence has become great and your dominion is far reaching. The messenger, the holy one, is ordering this tree, which is you, to be cut down and destroyed, but the stump of the tree and its roots are to remain, bound by a metal band, among the animals with the plants and get wet with the rain. What this means, O King, is the the Most High God is commanding my lord the king be banished from society of men and become as an animal. The stump of the tree with its roots is to remain so that you may know that you will be renewed and restored to your kingdom (Daniel 4:22-26 paraphrased).

Daniel urged the king to change his ways so he might have peace of mind.

Joseph and Daniel: Two Interpreters of Others' Dreams

> Although the issue has been determined and the sentence pronounced, there is something you can do. You can acknowledge God as supreme and decide to be kind to the oppressed, and it may be that you will be healed and your kingdom restored (Daniel 4:27).

However, King Nebuchadnezzar continued to behave as though his success were all his own doing, and he didn't give God any credit. In fact he set himself up as God. The result of this megalomania was seven years of insanity during which he ate grass like the cattle. He let his personal appearance get so terrible that his hair grew long as a goat's and his nails long like bird claws. The dream itself told the dreamer how he could change the situation if he chose to, and when he decided to open his life to God and acknowledge Him, he was restored and transformed back into a human, and he learned more about God and humankind and himself (Daniel 4:37).

Daniel dealt gently with the dreamer. At the same time he was honest and courageous in letting the dream speak the truth. King Nebuchadnezzar's dream pictured for him how he would change into a beast because he was acting so unreasonable and arrogant. But this was something nobody likes to be told about. He finally acknowledged the sovereignty of the Most High God and praised Him "for all his acts are right and his ways are just and those whose conduct is arrogant he can bring low" (Daniel 4:37). Again there was transformation. This time it was positive and there was healing and growth. The dreamer was not only personally restored and renewed, but was re-established in society with even greater influence.

Daniel was an excellent model of what it means to relate dreams to God and to use them to promote healing. He affirmed God as the source of wisdom, dreams, and dream interpretation. He responded to God with devotion.

Daniel also gives us the essentials of modern dream theory when he says, "The dream has come to you, O King, in order that you may know the thoughts of your inmost mind."[6]

Dreams about ill health are still common today. They help people recognize the inner thoughts that may be causing their illness or are related to it. Dr. Leslie Weatherhead, in his book

Part One: Dreams and Visions in the Hebrew Bible

Psychology in Service of the Soul, describes a dream in which a woman was shown how she could recover from her ill health. She was shown how to handle a situation that was causing the emotional stress that contributed to her ill health. In her dream the woman was standing under the cover of her porch. Her brother was in the middle of the road getting drenched in a raging storm. Eventually the dreamer ran out to her brother, threw her coat over him, and took him into her house. Dr. Weatherhead suggested that she make up with her brother. She was surprised because she hadn't mentioned that she and her brother had quarreled. But the doctor had studied dreams and knew that storms in dreams usually stand for emotional turbulence. From the context of the dream, the problem seemed to be with her brother. The rest of the dream tells her to do something to set things right and take him back into her life (house).

She did write him and invited him to visit her, and she was cured. Her feeling of guilt over leaving her brother to face his problem alone because of her self-righteous attitude had been making her sick. Her dream helped her understand the thoughts of her inmost mind and, like Nebuchadnezzar, pictured a solution to her problem. It is important to make a distinction here between dreams that give a solution and other dreams that define the problem and reflect only how the dreamer is dealing with it.

Daniel continued to dream and see visions. Four visions and their interpretations are described in the remainder of the Book of Daniel. In them he sees "the rise and fall of earthly kingdoms and finally the rise of an everlasting kingdom" (NEB notes). They are rich in imagery and symbols and are called apocalyptic visions. An apocalypse is a "preview of the end of one age and the establishment of another."[7] In this way it is akin to prophecy. Some consider them literary devices that give encouragement to the Jews in an era of oppression and persecution. Such writings were in symbols and words that could be understood by the persecuted but not by the oppressors, so even the interpretations are puzzling to us.

Joseph and Daniel: Two Interpreters of Others' Dreams

Chapter seven of the Book of Daniel begins by saying Daniel had the following dream:

> In the first year of Belshazzar king of Babylon, Daniel had a dream, and visions passed through his mind as he was lying on his bed. He wrote down the substance of his dream.

Daniel said "In my vision of night I looked and there before me were the four winds of heaven churning up the great sea. Four great beasts, each different from the others came up out of the sea."

Perhaps this is a mixture of visions while dreaming and visions while awake—deliberate, conscious, literary productions. Morton Kelsey reminds us that in keeping with the Hebrew tradition, Daniel speaks of dreams and visions in the same breath without distinction, nor does he distinguish between them by content. However, since they are lengthy, I will only summarize them. (This will necessitate my omitting much of the rich symbolism; therefore, I urge you to read in the Bible the entire portion covering these visions.)

Typical of apocalyptic writings, many symbols are various sorts of animals and creatures made up of parts of different animals. The parts represent certain qualities of the animals from which they were derived. There are four such beasts in the first vision/dream: a lion with eagle's wings that are suddenly plucked, a bear with ribs in its mouth, a winged leopard with four heads, a monster with iron teeth and ten horns plus a little horn that has the eyes of a man and a mouth that speaks proud words.

The scene shifts in a way that is typical of dreams and one "Ancient of Days" (God?) appears on a throne of flames with wheels of blazing fire. He wears a snow-white robe and his hair is like clean wool. A flowing river streams out before him. Thousands serve him and myriads attend him. He slays the fourth beast with the "little horn." The vision continues.

Part One: Dreams and Visions in the Hebrew Bible

> In my vision at night I looked, and there before me was one like a son of man, coming with the clouds of heaven. He approached the Ancient of Days and was led into his presence. He was given authority, glory and sovereign power, all peoples, nations and men of every language worshiped him. His dominion is an everlasting dominion that will not pass away, and his kingdom is one that will never be destroyed (Daniel 7:13-14).

So troubled and disturbed by all he is seeing, even Daniel, an interpreter of dreams, has to ask for meaning. This he does while remaining in the dream state, and the vision continues giving him an explanation of all that he has seen. The four beasts represent four kingdoms. This appears to be a review of history and provides the setting for the prediction that the "saints of the Most High" would eventually be saved. Again we find two characteristics we have already seen in many of the other dreams. There is conversation/dialogue within the dream/vision and interpretation provided by the vision. The dreamer is aware of being in a dream or vision and is able to remain in the vision while at the same time trying to understand it. Dreams in which there is cooperation between the dreaming self and the conscious self during the sleeping state are today called **lucid** dreams. This ability, the structure of the dream with shifting scenes, and the rich imagery all suggest to me that Daniel receives this vision as a dream, or had exceptional skill in devising literature with dreamlike characteristics.

The next three visions supplement and reinforce the message of the first.

In the second vision Daniel sees more animal imagery: a ram with two horns and a male goat with one horn between its eyes (a unicorn?). There is a fight between the two animals, and the goat wins. The goat's one horn is broken. Then a most unusual thing happens. The one horn is replaced by four more horns. From one of these four horns a "little" horn spouts and grows. It grows strong and arrogant and attacks even the stars of heaven and also the Jewish Temple. Then Daniel hears a holy voice predict that the atrocities will end and the sanctuary be

Joseph and Daniel: Two Interpreters of Others' Dreams

purified. The angel Gabriel interprets the vision to Daniel, but even then Daniel says "I was appalled by the vision; it was beyond understanding." He was so exhausted by the experience, he lay ill for several days before going on about his work.

The third vision comes to Daniel while he is praying for his people. He had been reading the scripture and reflecting on why the promise made to Jeremiah—that the Jews would be liberated after seventy years of captivity—had not been fulfilled. As he confesses and pleads for forgiveness on behalf of the people, the angel Gabriel appears and explains that Jeremiah's seventy years meant a longer period of time. Again he assures Daniel that God's judgment would fall upon the enemies of Jerusalem.

The fourth vision begins with a beautiful description of an angelic figure.

> I was standing on the bank of the great river, the Tigris. I looked up and here before me was a man dressed in linen, with a belt of the finest gold around his waist. His body was like chrysolite (topaz), his face like lightning, his eyes like flaming torches, his arms and legs like the gleam of burnished bronze, and his voice like to sound of a multitude (Daniel 10:4b-6).

Does this not sound like a description of an angel? The human figure with superhuman characteristics says he was in battle with the angel prince of Persia (Daniel 10:13, 21) and was aided by Michael, the guardian angel of Israel (Daniel 10:13, 12:1). This seems to identify him as an angel. This man/angel tells Daniel of events in history that had already happened as though they were about to happen. Then he tells Daniel of Michael and other heavenly beings who are protecting the Jews and says there will be further wars and distress, but assures him that there will be deliverance.

Deliverance takes on a new meaning in this vision and includes a clear concept of resurrection after death, which is unique in the Hebrew Bible.

Part One: Dreams and Visions in the Hebrew Bible

> Multitudes who sleep in the dust of the earth will awake; some to everlasting life, others to shame and everlasting contempt. Those who are wise will shine like the brightness of the heaven and those who lead many to righteousness, like the stars for ever and ever (Daniel 12:2-3).

Chapter 5

A Criminal's Vision and Conversation with God

> I was tending my father-in-law's flock of sheep on the far side of Mt. Horeb when I see a bush on fire that did not burn up. I went over to see this strange sight and pondered why the bush did not burn up, when I heard God say, "Do not come any closer. Take off your sandals, for the place where you are standing is holy ground. I am the God of your forefathers, Abraham, Isaac and Jacob. I have seen the misery of my people in Egypt—the brutality of the Egyptians toward them—and I have come to deliver them out of that land into a land flowing with milk and honey. I will send you and you shall bring my people Israel out of Egypt."

Dreamer: Moses
Source: paraphrase of Exodus 3:1-11

The Lord says in the Bible that he spoke to Moses mouth to mouth and not in dark speech (dreams and visions) as he did with the prophets (Numbers 12:6). This is probably because he had a different purpose for Moses to fulfill. This unusual visionary image was used to get Moses' atten-

Part One: Dreams and Visions in the Hebrew Bible

tion and to initiate him into a lifetime of being an "intimate confidant of God," to use a phrase from Robert Karl Gnuse (*The Dream Theophany of Samuel,* University of America, Inc., 1984). I include this visionary image because it is a fine example of conversation with God, which so often accompanied dreams as well as visions. Some writers refer to this as dialogue. I like to call it conversation. To me, *dialogue* seems more two-sided, while *conversation* suggests working together.

Moses' family were Hebrew slaves in Egypt.[8] Moses himself had fled to the Sinai desert after killing an Egyptian overseer. Now Moses is asked in a vision to return to Egypt. This visionary experience is important within the total history of the Hebrew people because it renewed the covenant with Abraham's descendants, who had become slaves. It launched the shaping of them into a nation in the wilderness, brought them to the border of the promised land, and established a religion that still flourishes.

Moses responded with conversation. If anyone believes the Biblical dreamer or visionary blindly followed orders or re-enacted actions of the dream or vision, they should pay attention to these conversations.

Bill and Carolyn Self, in addition to my own bus trip across the desert from Egypt to Jerusalem, have made Moses come alive for me. Using lines from the book of their experiences,[9] I've paraphrased this conversation as follows:

> MOSES: Who am I, a weather beaten old shepherd, that I should go to Pharaoh Rameses II who sits in gold armament on a throne with couriers all around him?
>
> GOD: I will be with you.
>
> MOSES: And the Israelites? Suppose I go to the Israelites and say, "The God of your fathers has sent me to you," and they ask me, "What is his name?" What is your name, God? Which name fits you? They have the god of the sun, and the god of the Nile, the god of the crops, the god of fertility, and all these other gods. I'm going to need some credentials.

A Criminal's Vision and Conversation with God

GOD: Tell them, "I AM has sent me to you. The God of Abraham, Isaac, and Jacob has sent me to you." This is my name forever, the name by which I am to be remembered from generation to generation. *(God outlines plans to follow and tells Moses what to expect from the Egyptians.)*

MOSES: *(Imagining how it will be standing before Pharaoh and the slaves saying, "I AM sent me to take his people out of bondage.")* What if they do not believe me or listen to me and don't believe that you appeared to me?

(God gives him signs to use.)

MOSES: O Lord, I have never been eloquent. I am slow of speech and tongue.

GOD: Who gave people their mouths? Is it not I, the Lord? I will help you speak and will teach you what to say.

MOSES: O Lord, I think it's a good thing to do. Somebody ought to do it, but please send someone else to do it.

GOD: What about your brother Aaron? I know he can speak well. I will help both of you and teach you what to do.

What a beautiful example of working together in conversation. The burning bush that didn't burn was certainly an attention-getter. However, it was not enough to convince an eighty-year-old escaped criminal with a speaking disability that he ought to go back to the scene of the crime and convince the ruler of the most powerful nation in the world to free his labor force. He had to be sure his imagination wasn't playing tricks on him. Talking it through helped Moses dispel his doubts and feelings of inadequacy and helped him get a picture of the plan. It wasn't just that he was reluctant; this was a monumental task, and he needed to be sure before he undertook such a commitment. Have you ever thought of a dream as an invitation to converse with one of its characters—or God?

Chapter 6

A Diviner's Dream Blesses God's People

> God came to me (in the night, Numbers 22:8) and said to me concerning the elders of Moab, "Do not go with those who have been sent to you to get you to curse the Israelites. You must not put a curse on those people because they are blessed...." Another group of men were sent to summon me to go with them, but God said, "Do only what I tell you."

Dreamer: Balaam
Source: Paraphrase of Numbers 22:12-20

Balaam was a diviner hired by the Moabites to deliver a curse on the Israelites as Moses led them across Moab on the way to Canaan from Egypt. As the result of the above dream and visionary experience, he blessed Israel instead.

Divination was the practice of gaining secret knowledge from gods or spirits by reading and interpreting certain signs called **omens**. Diviners were hired to pronounce curses, too. A curse was an expression of a wish that evil would befall one's

Part One: Dreams and Visions in the Hebrew Bible

enemies. One of the uses of a curse was for protection. Ancient people believed also that they could enlist the help of the deity and superhuman beings in carrying out curses.

A blessing carried the connotation of well-being and prosperity. God was understood to be the source of a blessing, although he gave it through an agent such as a priest, king, or head of a household. In this instance, due to divine intervention through means of a dream, a person outside the chosen people was the agent of the blessing.

The idea of a single God who was invisible, supreme, without death, independent of both nature and humankind, and who was responsive to humankind, was new among the tribes through which the Hebrew people were traveling. Certainly such a unique God could bless the custodians of this special way of thinking about Himself, mankind, and nature.

I have no experience with dreams for such a specific purpose. I do know that dreams instruct as this dream instructed Balaam. This dream helps me to be open to dreams that may instruct me for the well-being of another.

Chapter 7

A Midianite Soldier's Dream Predicts Victory for Israel

> I had a dream: A round loaf of barley bread came tumbling into the Midianite camp. It struck the tent with such force that the tent overturned and collapsed.

Dreamer: Midianite soldier, speaking to a comrade
Source: Judges 7:13b

The entire episode, the dream and its interpretation occurs in the camp of the enemy for whom it portends evil."[10] Barley was not an unusual staple fare in the common soldier's everyday life. But the action described was. The Midianite soldier tells his dream to a comrade, and it sounds very much like two friends discussing an ordinary dream; however, the comrade immediately gave an interpretation, so perhaps he was known to have this ability and that is why he was told the dream.

Part One: Dreams and Visions in the Hebrew Bible

The barley cake symbolizes "settled farmers" (NEB). He translates this image to be the sword of Gideon, who is the leader of the Israelites, who were now considered settled in Canaan. The tent symbolizes the "Nomadic Midianites"; the barley cake rolling into the tent and overturning it represents the sword of Gideon defeating their army. A discouraging dream prediction for the dreamer and interpreter, such as this was, probably served more as psychological preparation than a warning for what was to happen.

A most unusual aspect of this dream is that Gideon overhears it. Gideon has been directed by the Lord in the night to go to the enemy camp and listen to what they are saying. There he receives divine communication through what seemed to be a "chance utterance." Gideon had been very much afraid. Now, in the ways of his ancient Hebrew predecessors, he responds to the entire experience by worshiping God. Then he sets out in confidence for the task ahead of him. He recognized God's intervention in this strange turn of events.

Chapter 8

A Child's Scary Dream Has Far-reaching Implications

As I lay down to sleep I heard my name called. Thinking it was Eli, the elderly High Priest, with whom I lived in the Temple, I answered and ran to him saying, "Here I am, you called me." But Eli said he had not called and told me to go back and lie down. This happened two more times. The third time Eli told me once more to lie down. "This time," he said, "if he calls again say, 'Speak Lord, for your servant is listening.'" I did as I was instructed. The Lord came and stood there and I answered. Then the Lord said to me, "Behold, I am about to do this thing in Israel at which the two ears of everyone who hears it will tingle." Then he told me the fate of Eli and his two sons because the sons were blaspheming God and Eli did not restrain them. I lay until morning. I was afraid to tell Eli, and I knew he would ask. Just as I expected, he did ask and insisted that I tell him. All he said was, "He is the Lord. Let him do what is good in his eyes."

Dreamer: Samuel
Source: Paraphrase of I Samuel 3:2f.

Part One: Dreams and Visions in the Hebrew Bible

Samuel's confusion between external and internal experiences is not unusual for a young child. Young children are often not able to tell the difference between outer and inner reality. The following is a newspaper account of a five-year-old girl who had a similar experience.

The van her mother was driving plunged more than one hundred feet down a cliff. She and her mother were thrown out of the van. Her mother was critically injured. The child, who suffered a concussion and a deep cut on one arm, climbed that steep cliff in the dark and got help to her mother, who by then had been lying there for eight hours. The little girl, who stopped a passing motorist, told him that she had met a little boy with dark curly hair and a puppy. The boy had told her not to worry; she and her mother would be okay. Until then, she had thought her mother dead. The little girl said that after that meeting she fell and hit her head and spent the night in a hole on the cliffside. The terrain was too rough for another child to have been wandering about—especially during the night. It was so steep and rugged that it still doesn't seem possible this little girl ever got out. The paramedic who helped rescue her mother said, "I don't know what it was. I think that she saw him, whether she saw him in her mind or not." (*The Louisville Times*, June 18, 1986).

Also, Samuel's dream is an audition, a verbal message without imagery. Although Samuel's experience seems to be an auditory dream, he himself refers to it as a vision (1 Samuel 3:15). Again this is a case of using "dream" and "vision" interchangeably. His vision is a prediction and is fulfilled, launching Samuel as a prophet of the Lord (1 Samuel 3:20). He was the last of thirteen judges who ruled Israel. It was near the end of the time of Judges that Samuel became a judge while still a young boy.

The Bible says, "...Word from the Lord was rare and visions infrequent" (1 Samuel 3:1). Perhaps the people did not listen to them. We really do not know. Samuel became the first prophet and guided Israel through the first monarchy.

Chapter 9

A Prophet Dreams a Message for the King

> This is what the Lord almighty says...I will raise up your offspring to succeed you....He (your offspring) is the one who will build a house (temple) for my Name and I will establish the throne of his kingdom forever.

Dreamer: Nathan, speaking to King David
Source: 2 Samuel 7:8, 12b-13

David's response to this reassuring yet disappointing message was to pray. It was disappointing in that David himself had wished to build the Temple in Jerusalem, but reassuring in that it foretold that it would be built by his son and the kingdom would be established forever. Nevertheless, David expressed gratitude, even surprise, that the Lord was so gracious and generous in his dealings with mankind and with David himself. Truly this dream accomplished what the Law according to Deuteronomy said a dream correctly understood should do: bring the dreamer (sometimes others) into a closer relationship to the one living God.

Part One: Dreams and Visions in the Hebrew Bible

WHAT THE PROPHETS TAUGHT ABOUT DREAMS

The Israelite nation that David established split after Solomon's death. The northern kingdom was called Israel and gave only lip service to the God of Abraham, Isaac, Jacob, and Joseph, and they worshiped the gods and goddesses of Baal. This worship included the use of prostitutes in fertility orgies to promote increase in crops, livestock, and children. In times of crises, children were sometimes sacrificed. Those who protested were executed. The southern kingdom was called Judah. They cleansed the temple of other gods for brief periods, and they prided themselves on keeping the letter of God's law, believing this fulfilled their obligation to God.

A few brave visionaries, called prophets, tried without success to warn the kings and others of their folly. "Prophets were men who, on the basis of a particular and special revelation, announced God's word concerning his people, and other nations as well. They were preoccupied with declaring God's actions in the immediate future" (NEB, p. 12) The "special revelations" they declared were frequently from dream-like experiences. It is not clear whether they were dreams and visions during sleep, but the images and activity they saw needed interpreting and were clearly meant for the whole nation.

There were those who falsely claimed to have this ability. These false prophets were called "dreamers of dreams" and were strongly warned about in the Law (Deuteronomy 13).[11] False dream interpretation was part of the broader problem of false prophets. Priests of non-Hebraic people would lead the false prophets to some other gods, thus the Israelites were warned not to go to these priests with their dreams or to get information about the future (Deuteronomy 18:9-22). For the Israelites, using and interpreting dreams superstitiously was punishable by death (Deuteronomy 13:1-5).

A Prophet Dreams a Message for the King

The prophets of the God of Israel dealt with this problem. Ezekiel 13 discusses it as does Isaiah. Sometimes it seems on the surface that Isaiah and the other prophets were taking a negative view of dreams as revealed by God. Isaiah seems to hold dreams in low esteem when he refers to "people crouching among graves" to consult with the dead (NEB notes) and keeping vigil all night, long awaiting a dream revelation (NEB notes), and he includes them with other questionable acts. More than likely, he is denouncing the practices related to the dreams, not the dreams themselves.

Micah 3:5-7 describes prophets who would lead the people astray. At the same time, he warns that they may find themselves without instruction from God through dreams. Zechariah 10:2 refers to fake dreams and prophets (13:4). Jeremiah especially deals with the problem of false prophets and how to distinguish them from the true prophets of God.

A sermon by Weldon Gaddy, a minister friend, deals with the passages from Jeremiah. He discovers within the context of Jeremiah's prophecy a criteria for evaluating prophets and preachers.[12] It is helpful in identifying genuine dreams and visions. All scripture references are from the Book of Jeremiah.

Q. Toward whom or toward what are the prophets leading their listeners?
A. In Samaria prophets were leading people away from God (23:13).

Q. What do the prophets' lives look like? What do their own characters reveal?
A. In Jerusalem they commit adultery and walk in lies (23:14).

Q. Where do the prophets get their messages? What do they actually say?

Part One: Dreams and Visions in the Hebrew Bible

   A. There were prophets who proclaimed their own thoughts as divine will, who interpreted their own dreams and declared them to be God's word. They said only what the people wanted to hear.

   Q. Why are they in it (the vocation?) What motivates the prophets?
   A. Jeremiah asks "Who among them has stood in the council of the Lord?" (23:19) "Do you think you have exclusive rights on God?" (23:23).
   Q. What happens to the prophet's ministry? What becomes of the prophet's message?
   A. "...this is the most difficult. No immediate answer for it is available...only time will tell...by the time the identity of the true prophet is clearly revealed it is usually too late to change loyalties!" (18:24).

Nevertheless, today we are still encouraged to listen to the sermon and use discernment and never stop listening for the prophetic word. "Without that word, that voice, and that vision, there is no repentance, no encouragement for faithfulness, no guidance, no redemption." Dreams are part of that prophetic word.

The Book of Habakkuk offers some insight on the nature of visions that suggests to us how we might prepare to dream or to get insights of a visionary nature (2:1-3):

1. Get ready to receive one.
2. Expect to receive one.
3. Be open to receiving one.
4. Set yourself apart from turmoil of living.
5. Be alert as an attentive watchman for what God will say.
6. Don't be in a hurry.

The vision takes time to form. It comes from a place with its own time schedule. It will come at the right time. The task of the prophet is to make it known by writing it down.

A Prophet Dreams a Message for the King

The discussion about visions and prophets may not seem to apply to dreams until we remember that, in Hebrew Bible times, no distinction was made between them. Dreams were simply visions people saw while they were asleep. The important thing was the message, not the images or the manner in which it was received. There are many images and interpretations found in the writings of the prophets, and anyone interested in symbols would enjoy reading them. One interesting observation in the writings of Zechariah is that the interpretation is done by an angel through dialogue with the Lord.

Joel gives us a positive view of dreams related to prophecy and therefore prophets. He envisions a time, inaugurated by God's love (Joel 2:28) when the (Lord's) spirit, the animating force behind the prophets (NEB notes) is to come to all Israel and therefore be a possession of all people, men and women, young and old alike. He writes that God says "I will pour out my spirit on all people; your sons and your daughters will prophecy, your old men will dream dreams and your young men will see visions" (NIV).

Chapter 10

A Dream as a Source of Wisdom

God said, "What shall I give you? Tell me." I answered, "Living God, you have made your servant king in the place of my father, David, but I do not know how to carry out my duties....So give me the wisdom and knowledge I need to govern your people and to know right from wrong." The Lord was pleased and said to him, "You have made a good choice. I will give you wisdom and knowledge. And since you have not asked for riches and honor, nor for the death of your enemies, not for long life, I will also give you wealth, riches, and honor, too. There will never be anyone before you or after you with more wisdom and understanding and no king in your lifetime will have more riches and honor. And if you walk in my ways and obey my statutes and commands as David your father did, I will give you a long life." Then I awoke—and I realized I had been dreaming.

Dreamer: Solomon
Source: Paraphrase of 1 Kings 3:5-15, also 2 Chronicles 1:7-12

Solomon is the only king to receive a message directly from God by a dream. He had gone to Gibeon to the chief hill-shrine to worship with sacrifices at the Tent of

Part One: Dreams and Visions in the Hebrew Bible

God's Presence, which Moses had made in the wilderness (2 Chronicles 1:3 NEB). Perhaps Solomon sought to dream of guidance for the awesome task of being king over this new nation. Sleeping in a sacred place in order to receive divine help through a dream (incubation) was practiced by the kings of the Ancient Near East, although usually this was a function of the priests and prophets.[13]

This dream is reported entirely as dialogue, which is rare among the early incubated dream reports. Usually only the deity speaks, and then he addresses the sleeper like a parent, with the only reaction admitted to by the dreamer being one of submissive consent.[14]

Although this could be called a dialogue between God and Solomon, it sounds much like a prayer Solomon may have prayed while awake being repeated in the dream, this time with God's response. There is no working through of difficulties or making known a possibility that the dreamer had not previously been aware of on a conscious level.

Solomon responded by going to Jerusalem, where David had housed the Ark of the Covenant, and made offerings and held a feast for all his servants to celebrate God's coming to him and acting in a dream.

Twenty years later, after the Temple and the Royal Palace were built, God appeared to Solomon again "as in Gibeon" (I Kings 9:2), so apparently it was a dream. At that time God promised to protect the new Temple at Jerusalem and the Royal Palace, on the condition that he would follow only the Lord God. Solomon soon forgot this contact from outside the physical realm and failed to meet this condition, so things went downhill after his reign. However, God kept his promise of wisdom and wealth, and to this day we talk of Solomon's wisdom and recall the splendor of his reign.

Should we consider incubating dreams with a prayer or a worship experience? Solomon's first dream came at the beginning of his reign as king of a growing nation. The next dream came after he had accomplished the great undertaking that fulfilled David's hopes. These were crossroads in his life. Per-

A Dream as a Source of Wisdom

haps at such special times in our lives, it might be appropriate to seek help through a dream. When we seek help through a dream, we need to be aware that the dream answer may not be in keeping with our expectations any more than the way God answers our prayers is in keeping with our expectations.

Chapter 11

A Vision of God's Holiness

In the year that King Uzziah died, I saw the Lord seated on a throne, high and exalted, and the train of his robe filled the temple. Above him were seraphs, each with six wings. With two wings they covered their faces, with two wings they covered their feet, and with two they were flying. And they were calling to one another.

"Holy, holy, holy is the Lord Almighty;
the whole earth is full of his glory."

At the sound of their voices the doorposts and thresholds shook and the temple was filled with smoke.

"Woe to me!" I cried, "I am ruined! for I am a man of unclean lips, and I live among a people of unclean lips, and my eyes have seen the King, the Lord Almighty."

Then one of the seraphs flew to me with a live coal in his hand, which he had taken with tongs from the altar. "See, this had touched your lips; your guilt is taken away and your sin atoned for."

Then I heard the voice of the Lord saying, "Whom shall I send? And who will go for us?"

And I said, "Here am I. Send Me!"

Dreamer: Isaiah
Source: Isaiah 6:1-8

Part One: Dreams and Visions in the Hebrew Bible

The following discussion of Isaiah's experience is taken from *Great People of the Bible and How They Lived.*[15]

Isaiah's vision may have come to him when he was in his early twenties. Like many young adults in contemporary times, he had become increasingly sensitive to the corruption and injustices he observed in business, in the government, in the courts, and even in the priesthood. No doubt he felt frustrated and helpless to do anything significant about it. Then this profound emotional experience came to him.

Perhaps it was at the time of the coronation ceremony for the new king. The coronation was taking place at the time of the new-year festival. New Year's Day was the one time during the year when the eastern gates of the Jerusalem temple were unlocked. They were opened at dawn, when the rays of the rising sun could pass through and shine through the temple's doors. The whole courtyard would be lighted. Isaiah may have been among the worshipers who saw the gates swing apart as the early morning light appeared. What he physically saw is beautiful and soul-stirring in itself: sunlight streaming into the courtyard, across the great altar and the sanctuary, and Jotham, the new king, in purple robes embroidered with thread of gold, leading a solemn procession into this sunlit setting.

As magnificent as this experience was, Isaiah had this vision of a heavenly temple, which was even more majestic. It might have come to him during the event itself or shortly afterward. Just as the experiences of the day are often reflected in our dreams and thus used to give us further experiences, Isaiah's New Year's Day worship experience and the coronation may have been reflected in his vision of the holiness of God in the heavenly temple. It also set the scene for his own inaugural event, in which he is called to be God's spokesman.

Then again, a special occasion may not have been the background for this vision. It may have been the reflection of an ordinary visit to the temple. The elements of temple worship could have provided the imagery. God's "throne" was considered to be above the Ark in the temple (Exodus 25:18-22; Ezekiel 10:1-5); The "skirt of his robe" was possibly the cloud

A Vision of God's Holiness

of smoke that came from sacrifices and from the incense (2 Chronicles 7:1-3); the "seraphim" (fiery ones) are perhaps associated with the Ark (Ezekiel 1; Exodus 25:18-20); the seraph "covered his face" for fear of seeing God; the "smoke in the house" (the temple) should be associated with the "cloud" on Mount Sinai where "the glory of the Lord" was present (Exodus 19:9; Ezekiel 10:1-4).[16]

For the purposes of the Hebrew Bible, it isn't necessary to know the background of the vision. The important part is that he responds to it with great intensity. At first he responds within the vision with his feeling of unworthiness and is cleansed and purified still within the vision. Then he hears the Lord's asking for a messenger, and he replies with a lifelong commitment "Here am I; send me." Although Isaiah's commitment led to political involvement to save the nation and brought him such suffering and probably cost him his life, some believe his emphasis on God's holiness is "one of his most important contributions to the Hebrew-Christian conception of the Deity."[17] Certainly he remained true to his vision all the days of his life as advisor to kings and as a powerful religious spokesman whose language was as poetic and beautiful as his vision.

Summary of Dreams and Visions in the Hebrew Bible

As stated earlier, the dreams in the Hebrew Bible follow the pattern discovered in the Ancient Near East. When the dreamers were kings, priests, and professional dreamers, the dreams were considered divine messages and were recorded as official dreams in a manner that restricted and censored the content. The Ancient Hebrew dreamers mostly reported dreams with divine messages and predictions, and there are few references to dreams that reflect the dreamer's state or circumstances, such as hopes, needs, or conflicts, that would be of interest to dream specialists today.[18]

There are differences, however between the dreams of the ancient Hebrews and dreams of the rest of the Ancient Near East. The ancient Hebrews (and later Israelites) focused on the *message* of the content instead of the experience of dreaming. It made no difference whether the message came from dreams and visions, or nature, or society, or historical events. What was important was what it could reveal about the non-physical world (spiritual realm) as it related to the physical world—about God as He relates to humankind. Perhaps this is why the prophets put so much emphasis on the proper understanding of the dreams and were admired for their insight about God.

Part One: Dreams and Visions in the Hebrew Bible

Another characteristic of the Hebrew Bible dream reports is conversations between the dreamer and the deliverer of the dream message, who might have been God, an angel, or some other being considered a holy messenger. In these dreams, not only did God speak, but the dreamer answered either in the dream or afterward. There is as much reported on the conversation as is on the images. Conversing with God was one of the ways of understanding the significance of the dream message. Other ways were by means of an interpreter and by instantaneous understanding.

With the exception of the highly symbolic dreams of the non-Hebrew dreamers, who held dreams to be more in the realm of magic and needed the wise man/interpreter to understand the message, the Hebrew Bible dreamers appear to understand the meaning of the dream during the dreaming process itself. Perhaps the latter were free of the judgmental attitude in the conscious state that might prevent them from being open to the meaning presented by the dream, while the former did not have this open state of mind. In our present-day dreamwork, we frequently discover that a closed mind-set may prevent ideas from coming to the surface as we deal with the dream on a conscious level. One person may approach a dream in an open, relaxed way, making no effort to control thoughts regarding it, not forcing thoughts or trying to make it fit some preconceived notion. Another may approach it with doubt and fear, or exert too much effort, thus blocking thinking. This is akin to the anxiety we feel as we approach an examination at school or an evaluation on the job.

Besides valuing the message and the guidance of the dream, the Ancient Hebrews seemed to derive inspiration, healing, and growth from the total experience of the dream and the accompanying events surrounding it over a period of time. All this was attributed to the goodness of God drawing the dreamer into a closer relationship with Him and at the same time enhancing God's mystery.

Summary of Dreams and Visions in the Hebrew Bible

Although the Hebrew Bible dreams are not considered psychological status dreams, there is the element of emotion in many dream experiences.[19] Anxiety is frequently the emotional context of the dream, and most responses to the dreams by the dreamer are emotion-centered. Guilt, religious awe, anxiety, and assurance are some of the emotional responses. However, some responses are action-centered and some are a combination of emotion and action.[20] So though the dreams seem to be part of God's plan for founding and establishing a nation and a religion by which to bless the world, and deal with guidance and protection of Israel, they also testify to the deep personal concerns of the individual and give evidence of a faith in a living, caring God. "Thus, the dream is important in the understanding of humankind in the Hebrew Scriptures,"[21] as well as the understanding of God and what he is trying to do in the world.

Part Two
Dreams and Visions in the Apocrypha

Chapter 12

Dreams in the Intertestamental Period

Writings during this time indicate that dreams, angels, and visions continued to be considered one way God spoke to people. These writings are called the Apocrypha[1] and were found in the Greek translation. They were not included in the Hebrew Bible, but were used by the Christian church until the time of the Reformation. After that they were not included in the Protestant Bible, but some were kept in the Catholic Bible. They are useful because they act as a link between the Hebrew Bible and the New Testament and shed light on understanding both.[2]

Dreams and visions are dealt with in six of the Apocrypha books: 2 Esdras, Tobit, Esther (the Greek version), Wisdom of Solomon, Ecclesiasticus, and 2 Maccabees.

Ecclesiasticus 34:1-7 presents a negative view of dreams, though the writer acknowledges that some dreams come from the Most High (God) and deserve serious consideration.[3] Rather than a condemnation of dreams, this negative view may be in keeping

Part Two: Dreams and Visions in the Apocrypha

with the practice of distinguishing between ordinary dreams and message dreams from God. Otherwise, dreams continue to be valued by the Israelites as one way God communicated with humankind during this period. We find this attitude evident in the dream accounts from 2 Esdras and the Greek version of Esther.

In 2 Esdras, there is a very long account of dreams and visions and visits of the angel Uriel to Ezra, who was chief priest. The angel has been sent by the Most High God to comfort Ezra, who is deeply troubled by a difficult question that had previously bothered Job and continues to be a problem to us today. The popularity of a recent book, *Why Bad Things Happen to Good People* by Harold S. Kushner, is evidence that we are still troubled by the same question: Why do God's righteous people suffer? Ezra asks "why Adam's sin has been transmitted to his descendants, and why, therefore, all men have an inborn tendency toward evil....Uriel points out that Ezra cannot understand even the simple things in his own life—the weight of fire, the measuring of the wind, where past days go. How, then can he expect to understand the ways of God? In the great age to come, Uriel says, Ezra will be given the answers."[4]

There are more questions and discussion, and then the continued longing for a Messiah, which connects the Hebrew Bible and the New Testament. Uriel speaks of the Messiah (7:28) and shows Ezra a splendid new city, the New Jerusalem (10:27, 55b). Then the angel promises him visions in dreams of what would happen in the last days to the inhabitants of earth. Ezra tells his dream in great detail. Because it is so long, it has been paraphrased with excerpts from the Oxford Study Edition of the New English Bible with the Apocrypha. The entire passage should be read to fully understand why, at the end of the dream, the writer had reason to say he was utterly exhausted. An eagle is the first image Ezra sees.

> On the second night I had a vision in a dream; I saw, rising from the sea, an eagle with twelve wings and three heads. I saw it spread its wings over the whole earth; all the winds blew on it, and the clouds gathered. Out of its wings I saw rival wings sprout, which proved to be

Dreams in the Intertestamental Period

only small and stunted. Its heads lay still; even the middle head, which was bigger than the others, lay still between them. As I watched, the eagle rose on its wings to set itself up as ruler over the earth and its inhabitants...I saw the eagle stand erect on its talons and it spoke aloud to its wings...I saw that the sound was not coming from its heads, but from the middle of its body (2 Esdras 11:1-5, 7, 10).

The dream continued with all the wings taking on identities of their own and establishing successive reigns, so there were wings appearing and disappearing except for two little wings that stayed with the head on the right. Then the large head in the middle awoke and devoured two wings and established a powerful, oppressive worldwide kingdom, then vanished. The two remaining heads seized power, and the one head on the right devoured the other. At that point a new image emerged.

I looked and saw what seemed to be a lion roused from the forest; it roared as it came, and I heard it address the eagle in a human voice. "Listen to what I tell you," it said. "The most High says to you: 'Are you not the only survivor of the four beasts to which I gave the rule over my world, intending through them to bring my ages to their end? You are the fourth beast, and you have conquered all who went before, ruling over the whole world and holding it in the grip of fear and harsh oppression. The Most High has surveyed the periods he has fixed: they are now at an end, and his ages have reached their completion. So you, eagle, must now disappear and be seen no more, you and your terrible great wings, your evil small wings, your cruel heads, your grim talons, and your whole worthless body'....Then the eagle's entire body burst into flames and the earth was struck with terror.

Ezra awoke exhausted, saying "The terrors of this night have completely drained my strength." He was so alarmed that he prayed for strength and for an exact interpretation. A voice told him that the eagle represented the fourth kingdom described by Daniel (Daniel 7:7-8:23), and that the lion was God's promised Messiah. Then Ezra was told to write down all he had seen, but to tell only those wise enough to understand them and keep them safe.

Part Two: Dreams and Visions in the Apocrypha

Ezra dreamed again and saw a human figure rising from the sea (2 Esdras 13:1-11). Again the voice of the Most High interpreted what he has seen:

> The man you saw rising from the depths of the sea is he whom the Most High has held in readiness through many ages; he will himself deliver the world he has made, and determine the lot of those who survive. As for the breath, fire, and storm that you saw pouring from the mouth of the man so that without a spear or any weapon in his hand he destroyed the hordes advancing to wage war against him, this is the meaning: [The details are explained, and then:] my son will convict for their godless deeds the nations that confront him. This will correspond to the storm you saw. He will taunt them with their evil plottings and the tortures they are soon to endure. This corresponds to the flame. And he will destroy them without effort by means of the law—and that is like the fire.

"My lord, my master," I asked, "explain to me why the man that I saw rose up out of the depths of the sea." He replied: "It is beyond the power of any man to explore the deep sea and discover what is in it; in the same way no one on earth can see my son and his company until the appointed day" (2 Esdras 13:25b-28, 37-38, 51-52).

Ezra's dreams were highly symbolic and scary. He prayed to the Most High for understanding, and he believed that God gave the understanding directly after the dream. Then he took action. He rewrote the sacred books and prophesied to the people. Again we see in Ezra's experiences that dreams and visions are dealt with as though they were the same and that the angel and the Lord are used interchangeably.

Chapter 13

A Persian Queen's Cousin Saves God's People

This was the dream; din and tumult, peals of thunder and an earthquake, confusion upon the earth. Then appeared two great dragons, ready to grapple with each other, and the noise they made was terrible. Every nation was roused by it to prepare for war, to fight against the righteous nation. It was a day of darkness and gloom, with distress and anguish, oppression and great confusion upon the earth. And the whole righteous nation was troubled, dreading the evils in store for them, and they prepared for death. They cried aloud to God; and in answer to their cry there came as though from a little spring a great river brimming with water. It grew light and the sun rose; the humble were exulted and they devoured the great.

Speaker: Mardochaeus
Source: Esther 11:5-12 (NEB)

Part Two: Dreams and Visions in the Apocrypha

The dreamer of this dream is Mardochaeus (in Hebrew, Mordecai), Queen Esther's cousin. He was a Hebrew living in exile in Babylonia. Like Daniel, he was a man of high rank in the royal service.

The dream is apocalyptic in nature, with the imagery of dragons in a cosmic setting and God's promise of deliverance for God's chosen people. After Mardochaeus awoke, he tried all day to understand it.

At that time, a series of political events had taken place in which Haman, another person in high office, plotted against the Jews. He arranged for the extermination of the Jews and Mardochaeus because Mardochaeus had discovered a conspiracy to assassinate the king. Esther interceded and revealed the plot, so Haman and his followers are hanged instead. After all of this happened, Mardochaeus understood his dream and he said, "All this is God's doing."

> For I have been reminded of the dream I had about these things: not one of the visions I saw proved meaningless. There was the little spring which became a river, and there was light and sun and water in abundance. The river is Esther, whom the king married and made queen; the two dragons are Haman and myself; the nations are those who gathered to wipe out the Jews; my nation is Israel, which cried aloud to God and was delivered (Esther 10:4-9 NEB).

Reading this ancient dream account reminds me of something Henry Reed says in his "Personal Story." He believes dream interpretation is the art of fully remembering the dream. Recapturing the total understanding that must have accompanied the original dream experience takes time and practice in dreamwork techniques. Allowing time for the dream to have its effect in life can result in the meaning of the dream being realized and understood, thus the dream will no longer require interpretation.[5] This was Mardochaeus' experience.

Haven't we all, after a period of time, looked back on a dream and understood it when at first we did not? I will mull over a dream and my dreamwork experiences before arriving at a full understanding of it. Often this means just being aware of what

A Persian Queen's Cousin Dreams and Saves God's People

the dream has brought to my attention and observing what is going on in my life and around me. Dreams have a way of helping us to be more observant. Perhaps this is how the dream prepares us for certain events, and when they happen we recognize them as having been in our dream, and we are not so surprised. Our surprise comes from the fact that we've dreamed it.

Summary of Dreams and Visions in the Apocrypha

The last two chapters dealt with symbolic dreams; however, no interpreter—at least no earthly one—was required. In the first dream, the interpretation was given with the dream. In the second, the events following the dream led the dreamer to understanding, and the dreamer gave God the credit.

The centuries-old concerns about suffering, about the struggle between evil and good, and about the long-awaited Messiah continued to be reflected in these dreams. Not only did the Jewish people continue to appreciate dreams, but they continued to believe that this was one way God spoke to them.

Part Three
Dreams and Visions in the New Testament

Chapter 14

Historical Background of New Testament Dreams

The same reverence for dreams continued in late Jewish literature. The Talmud, the Hebrew book second in authority after the Bible, describes dreams as breakthroughs into human reality from the world of the spirit or from God himself. The Talmud encourages the understanding of these dreams.

Dreams continued to be valued even after the Greek culture was introduced into the Near Eastern countries with the coming of the Greek conquerors and Alexander the Great. The Greeks valued dreams as much as the Hebrews did and treated them with reverence. They also believed that dreams were intrusions of a non-human or a more-than-human source, and they regarded them as divine communication. The Greeks considered the irrational aspects to be as real as the rational, although they placed more emphasis on the rational. They practiced dream incubation

Part Three: Dreams and Visions in the New Testament

for medical purposes in their temples. They valued the dream, vision, and trance equally. They did not evaluate their dreams as critically as the Hebrews did.

The writers of the New Testament didn't distinguish between true and false dreams as did the writers of the Hebrew Bible. This may be because the New Testament writers still relied on the Hebrew Bible's teachings and felt no need to discuss the matter further (although, the impact of the Persian culture's different way of dealing with evil comes through in the writing). The dream (and vision) itself was considered real, but dreams are now classified as good or bad, depending on what spiritual power gave it. "...good dreams and visions were attributed to God, the Spirit, or angels, while the lying, the negative, or bad ones were seen as the result of demonic activity or infiltration rather than the creation of a false prophet."[1]

By the time of the birth of Jesus, many Jews were yearning even more strongly for the coming of a "heavenly one" who would deliver them from their pagan rulers. The prophets had foretold that this special one, the Messiah, would establish his kingdom over the whole earth. They disagreed as to how he would do this, but they believed that the Messiah would be a descendant of their beloved King David.

Only half of the population of Palestine was Jewish at this time, and Jews were split into many sections. They all resented the presence of a pagan culture in their ancient homeland. To the Jews their religion was more than a form of worship. It had to do with their very identity and the special place they believed the Lord had given them in history. The Jews alone worshiped a single, invisible God whom they believed to be more powerful than pagan gods in visible forms, called "graven images."[2]

Through all the foreign invasions, occupations, and the exile, they emphasized more and more those traditions and practices that set them apart, and they became intolerant of people they considered unclean (religiously impure). Their religious advisors spent much time discussing the religious laws and arguing among themselves. In the midst of all this, a baby's birth was announced through dreams and angels.

Chapter 15

A Foster Father-to-be Dreams

> When Joseph awoke from his sleep, he did as the angel of the Lord directed him and took her as his wife, but did not live with her as a husband until she had had a son; and he named Him Jesus.

Source: Matthew 1:24-25 (WNT)

This passage seems to portray Joseph as blindly carrying out the directions given in the dream. Let's back up a bit and put this dream in context.

First of all, Joseph already knew that Mary was to become the mother of a baby that wasn't his. He responded to this in the kindest way he thought possible and in a way that would protect the baby's life. He could have had Mary stoned to death according to religious law, but instead, not wishing to disgrace her, he had decided quietly to break the engagement and send her away. The dream now invites him to think of a third possibility. He could accept her as his wife, thus declaring to the community that he chose to be her husband despite her apparent act of adultery. He responded to the situation with

Part Three: Dreams and Visions in the New Testament

"the (Christian) principles of love and forgiveness and acceptance and chose to protect Mary and the baby by taking her to be his wife."[3]

Now, his decision to take Mary as his wife, thus accepting the job of rearing her son as he would his own, was a difficult one. There is no report of a conversation with the angel over this, but he obviously had to deal with his feelings and values. How would this look to others? What should he think of Mary? What did the religious law say? He must have done a lot of talking to himself despite the angel's assurance that he need not be afraid.

God often told people in dreams not to be afraid. God wants us to live out of love—not fear. Our dreams can help us be more loving. One author who writes about dreams says that by learning to love the monsters in his dreams, he learned to practice Jesus' teaching, "Love your enemies." Should we not look to our dreams for ways of practicing love and care in our relationships?

Joseph continued to use his dreams as guidance in protecting the infant's life.

> ...An angel of the Lord appeared to (me), Joseph, in a dream and said "Wake up! Tenderly take the child and his mother, and escape to Egypt; stay there until I further direct you, for Herod is going to search for the child to destroy him" (Matthew 2:13-14 WNT).

> ...an angel of the Lord in a dream appeared to (me), Joseph, in Egypt, and said, "Wake up, tenderly take the child and his mother, and make the trip to the land of Israel, for those who sought the child's life are dead" (Matthew 2:19-20 WNT).

> But because I heard that Archelaus was ruling over Judea in the place of his father, Herod, I was afraid to go there; and because I was divinely warned in a dream, I set out for the region of Galilee...to Nazareth and made our home there. (Matthew 2:22-23 WNT paraphrased in first person).

A Foster Father-to-be Dreams

No images were described except that of an angel, but that angel was someone very real, in a visionary sense, whom Joseph saw and heard.[4] These dream messages required no interpretation. No chances of wrong interpretations were taken with the life of baby Jesus. "None of the dreams of the New Testament needed an interpretation."[5] And the infant's life was protected not only by his foster father's dream, but by a dream to the wise men of the East.

> Then (after they had worshiped the child and presented gifts to him), as we had been divinely warned in a dream not to return to Herod, we set out to our country by another route (Matthew 2:12 WNT, paraphrased in first person).

Chapter 16

Jesus and Dreams

> I most solemnly say to you, whoever does not enter the sheepfold by the door, but climbs over at some other place is a thief and a robber. But the one who enters by the door is the shepherd of the sheep. The doorkeeper opens the door to him, and the sheep obey his voice; and he calls his own sheep by name, and leads them out. So when he gets his sheep all out, he goes on before them, and the sheep come on behind him, because they know his voice. But they will never come on behind a stranger, but will run away from him, because they do not know the voice of strangers (Jesus in John 10:1-6.)

We have no record of Jesus' dreams. This is a story Jesus told. He told many such stories called parables. They remind us of dreams because he uses objects, persons, and events from the physical world to teach a truth about the spiritual world. Jesus is at home equally in both the physical and spiritual, according to the New Testament narrative of his life. There are those today who say, "Tales of dreams suggest that dreaming and waking partake of the same reality which is both spiritual and physical."[6] Jesus demonstrates this. Certainly if God saw fit to communicate with Moses directly rather than in dreams (Numbers 12:6),

Part Three: Dreams and Visions in the New Testament

he could do the same with Jesus, of whom he said, "This is my son, whom I love; with whom I am well pleased" (Matthew 3:17).

As we have seen, Jesus' birth and the important experiences of his life were accompanied by dreams, angels, visions, and other non-human interventions. "Jesus wholly and completely accepted the existence of a spiritual world and its power to effect the physical one."[7] This shows in his dealing with demons and evil spirits and in his teachings about angels.[8]

Sometimes Jesus explained his stories much as one interpreted dreams. In the story related here, he explains that the door of the sheepfold is himself; the thieves and robbers are false Messiahs or those who claim to be him; the sheep are followers; the good shepherd is himself; the stranger and the hired man are themselves.

Jesus retells this story with these representations much as we sometimes retell dreams after we've worked through them.

> I most solemnly say to you, I am the door of the sheepfold myself. All who came as such before me are thieves and robbers, but the true sheep would not listen to them. I am the door myself. Whoever enters through me will be saved, and will go in and out and find pasture. A thief does not come for any purpose but to steal and kill and destroy; I have come for people to have life and to have it till it overflows. I am the good shepherd myself. The good shepherd gives his own life for his sheep. The hired man, who is not a shepherd and does not own the sleep, sees the wolf coming and leaves the sheep and runs away, and the wolf carries off some of the sheep and scatters the flock. This is because he is a hired man and does not care a straw for his sheep. I am the good shepherd myself. I know my sheep and my sheep know me (Jesus in John 10:6-14)

Other people who appear in his stories are children, laborers, a sower, vineyard owners, servants, a householder, a king, and a landowner. Events and activities in his stories are wedding feasts, banquets, sowing seeds, hiring laborers, buying and selling, sorting and separating. He also speaks of flowers, birds,

Jesus and Dreams

trees, vines, salt, light, buried gold, money, lost coins, lost sheep, yeast, bread, houses, and roads. Picturesque images catch your attention:

- rusty, moth-eaten treasure
- a plank in an eye
- pigs trampling pearls
- two roads of different widths
- wolves wearing sheepskins
- a house built on rocks standing against floods and the wind
- a house built on sand crashing in the floods and wind
- a tidy house inhabited with unclean spirits
- a merchant selling all he has for one pearl of great price
- a net full of every kind of fish being sorted out
- blind leading the stumbling into a ditch
- a camel passing through the eye of a needle
- a rejected cornerstone
- improperly dressed wedding guests
- lawyers and Pharisees wearing large tassels on their robes, straining gnats out of their drinks but gulping down a camel

Don't all of these things sound like the stuff dreams are made of? Could Jesus, too, be the giver of dreams?

Chapter 17

The Apostles and Dreams

Dreams continued to be an important means of communication, this time between God and the apostles. The apostles were chosen by Jesus to establish the church, just as the forebears in the Hebrew Bible days were chosen by God to be his servants to bless all the people of the world down through the ages.

A VISION CHANGES THE ATTITUDE TOWARD NON-JEWISH BELIEVERS

The following is a dream/trance that Peter relates to the Jewish believers in Jerusalem. The full text is found in Acts 11:5-11.

> I was in the city of Joppa praying, and in a trance I saw a vision. I saw something like a large sheet being let down from heaven by its four corners, and it came down to where I was. I looked into it

Part Three: Dreams and Visions in the New Testament

> and saw four-footed animals of the earth, wild beasts, reptiles, and birds of the air. Then I heard a voice telling me, "Get up, Peter. Kill and eat." I replied, "Surely not, Lord! Nothing impure or unclean has ever entered my mouth." The voice spoke from heaven a second time. "Do not call anything impure that God has made clean." This happened three times, and then it was all pulled up to heaven again. Right then three men who had been sent to me from Caesarea stopped at the house where I was staying.

Dreamer: Peter
Source: paraphrase of Acts 11:5-11

This dream is very important to non-Jewish believers. It is not about changing dietary laws; it is about changing attitudes. Until now the Jewish people had not considered the possibility of the Messiah being also for the Gentiles, or pagans. This dream, along with a special set of circumstances,[9] helped to open Peter's mind to the possibility that God planned to bless all people with the Messiah. It took a special set of circumstances to get this through to Peter because he was obedient to Jewish religious practices. Perhaps Jesus had planted the thought in Peter's subconscious thinking when he taught, "I have other sheep, which are not of this fold, I must bring them also" (John 10:16).

The dream/trance was not only for Peter but for the greater community of Jewish believers in Jesus as the Messiah, and Peter had the task of helping them to understand this new insight about the Messiah.

In the above passage, Peter himself reports the experience of the dream/trance he had at Joppa (Acts 10), which resulted in his accepting an invitation from a gentile in Caesarea. The Jewish believers in Jerusalem were disturbed over the reports of his visiting and eating with gentiles/heathens/pagans (Acts 11:2-3). After hearing of this dream/trance and of the supernatural events accompanying it, they were willing to accept the non-Jews as believers. That was how greatly they respected the place of dreams in their religious lives.

The Apostles and Dreams

As we've observed about most biblical dreams, this dream is also part conversation. Peter talks with "the voice" about the images he sees and what they mean. He doesn't immediately understand its implications for himself or others (Acts 10:17). He needs further help from "the Spirit."[10]

Sometimes we have dreams, usually of an everyday nature, which are difficult to understand, especially for those not accustomed to thinking about their dreams. When we do all that we know to do, we find we need additional help, especially when the dream is one we can't seem to put out of our minds. Talking it over with an intuitive friend may be enough. Talking it over with God—is that a possibility you've thought of?

Just as Jacob grew as a person and as a leader in response to his ladder and angel dream, Peter grew both as a person and as a leader in the way he responded. He drew others into his religious community and led still others to include those they had been excluding.

We will often find that our ordinary dreams are of value to others. Some dreams will help us to relate to others for our own well-being and for the well-being of others. Some dreams may call our attention to community needs, especially among those we don't consider "one of us." Dreams can be important in transforming our attitudes toward others, just as it was with Peter.

Chapter 18

Night Visions Lead to the Expansion of Christianity

Dreams played a crucial role in the spread of early Christianity. As we have seen, a dream helped Peter and the Jewish believers to include Gentiles. Now Paul is directed to take Christianity into the Western World instead of Asia as he had planned.

> I, Paul, had a vision one night: A man from Macedonia kept standing and pleading with me in these words, "Come over to Macedonia and help us!" As soon as I had this vision, we laid our plans to get off to Macedonia... (Acts 16:9- 10, paraphrase).

This dream/night vision is special in two ways: first, for its role in expanding Christianity to the non-Jews; second, for its role in directing the movement of Christianity into the West. A third interesting possibility is its suggestion of group interpretation, which would be different in technique from other biblical interpretations.

Part Three: Dreams and Visions in the New Testament

We find Saul/Paul, who had once given all his energy to putting down the spread of Christianity, now putting his all into extending it into the farthest parts of his known world, which he thought at the time to be Asia. However, in Troas these plans are frustrated and he had this dream, which suggested an alternative action. Probably in Troas he saw Macedonian travelers from Southeast Europe, but may not consciously have given thought to going there with the message of Jesus. Going to sleep in frustration and putting his conscious mind-set at rest, Paul heard through his subconscious God speak to him of other places and other possibilities. The Macedonian man may have already come to his attention, but it took the dream to get his undivided attention and put his wish to help others know Jesus together with the people of Macedonia.

"We laid our plans to get off to Macedonia..." suggests the group worked together on the meaning of the dream, and certainly on the action in response to the meaning of the dream. Luke and Paul had in some way come together in Troas; there were others present, thought to be Silas and Timothy; and they all agreed on the meaning and action to be taken. Dream-sharing groups of today may be more biblical than we suppose.

Imagery in New Testament dream accounts are scarce. Peter's vision in the dream/trance, the appearance of angels, and this dream of the man from Macedonia are all that we have. This does not mean they did not see images and symbolic material in their dreams. The writers may have chosen to relate only the meaning understood by the dreamer. Then again, dreams are as individual as persons and as varied as their purposes. The dreamers may have needed clear messages without the confusion of symbols and imagery; however, I feel that because of their already committed lives to Jesus and his teachings, they were in a more open state of mind to accept information. The New Testament narrative doesn't really require the discussion of images, but the mention of them suggests the continuation of them from the Old Testament traditions.

Night Visions Lead to the Expansion of Christianity

Even in this dream narrative, we are only told that the man was from Macedonia. We don't know whether he is a Macedonian. We don't know whether the man is someone Paul knows or has at least seen. This was Paul's first visit to Troas, a seaport city across from Macedonia in Southeastern Europe. No doubt he saw Macedonian merchants and seamen, and something about them made an impression, but he didn't elaborate.

When Paul arrived in Phillipi, Macedonia, no particular man came to him as happened with Peter's dream/vision. Nor did he have a particular place to go. On the Sabbath he went to a place of prayer by the river and found women meeting. Instead of a man, it turned out to be a woman named Lydia, who was already a worshiper of God, who sought further knowledge of the Messiah. She declared, "I am a real believer in the Lord...." Another woman, a slave girl with the gift of fortune telling, recognized Paul and his companions as "Slaves of the Most High God" with the message of salvation. Because she kept shrieking after them, Paul commanded the evil spirit to leave her, which it did. As a result, Paul and Silas were beaten, jailed, and tortured, so that they finally left Phillipi. Lydia's household and the jailer with his household all became followers of Jesus, and a Christian community developed because of these experiences. Later Paul wrote a letter of joy to this congregation of believers.

Paul and his companion responded to the whole dream experience and did not act on just the visual part: searching for a particular man. Instead Paul related to the message "Come over...help us," and *us* included the Macedonian women.

> One night in a vision I, Paul, heard the Lord say, "Stop being afraid, go on speaking, never give up; because I am with you, and no one is going to attack you so as to injure you, because I have many people in this city." So I settled down among the Corinthians and went on teaching God's message (Acts 18:9-11 WNT paraphrased in first person).

Part Three: Dreams and Visions in the New Testament

Anxiety and fear were the main background emotions in Paul's above dream, whereas frustration had been the emotion in his Macedonia dream. Paul faced opposition in Corinth, but his night visions encouraged him to speak and reassured him that there were people in Corinth who would sympathize with his work. Paul was so strengthened by God's assurance of favor that he remained eighteen months at Corinth and laid a firm foundation of doctrine with his teaching.

When a conspiracy to kill Paul took place in Jeruslaem, he had the following dream:

> That same night the Lord (Jesus) stood by my side saying, "Courage! For as you have testified for me in Jeruslaem, you must testify for me in Rome, too" (Acts 23:11 WNT, paraphrase).

Dreams continued to encourage and direct Paul as we see in the dream below, which came to him during a shipwreck on the way to Rome.

> Just last night an angel of God, to whom I belong and whom I serve, stood by my side and said, "Stop being afraid, Paul. You must stand before the Emperor; and listen! God has graciously given to you the lives of all who are sailing with you" (Acts 27:23-24 WNT).

The following observations can be made concerning Paul and his dreams:

1. Paul took his dreams seriously and listened to them with great care.[11]
2. God guides those who belong to him through dreams (Acts 16:9).[12]
3. The Lord consoles and strengthens his disciples even by means of dreams (Acts 18:9; 24:11, 27:23f.).[13]
4. Paul used his dreams for the benefit of others, even those who guarded him as a prisoner (Acts 27:23-24).

Night Visions Lead to the Expansion of Christianity

No mention of Paul is complete without mentioning one last item. It is due to a day (waking) vision he has on the way to Damascus that he changes from an enemy to a believer in Christianity. This vision is a source of a conviction and faith so powerful that it brings about the conversion of the Greeks. We can feel this strength in this quotation from his letter to the church in Rome.

> For I am persuaded that neither death nor life, nor angels, nor principalities, nor powers, nor things present, nor things to come, nor height, nor depth, nor any other creature, shall be able to separate us from the love of God, which is in Christ Jesus our Lord (Romans 8:38 KJV).

Chapter 19

Visions of an Exiled Early Christian Leader

The following passages are taken from the Williams New Testament version of the Bible.

First Vision (Revelation 1:9-3:33)

I, John, your brother and companion with you in the trouble, the kingdom, the patient endurance which Jesus gives, found myself on the island called Patmos, for preaching God's message and testifying to Jesus. On the Lord's day I was in the Spirit's power and I heard a voice like a trumpet behind me say:

"Write what you see in a book and send it to the seven churches...." I turned to see who it was that was speaking to me, and as I turned I saw seven golden lampstands, and among the lampstands One resembling the Son of Man, wearing a robe that reached to his feet, and with a belt of gold around His breast. His head and hair were as white as white wool, as white as snow. His eyes were like coals of fire; His feet were like bronze refined to white heat in a furnace, and His voice was like the roar of many waters.

Part Three: Dreams and Visions in the New Testament

> In His right hand he was holding seven stars, and a sharp, double-edged sword was coming out of His mouth, and His face was shining like the sun at midday. So when I saw Him, I fell at His feet like a dead man. But He laid His right hand upon me and said: "Do not be afraid anymore. I am the First and Last: yea, the ever-living One. I once was dead, but now I live forever and ever. I carry the keys of death and the underworld." So write what you have seen, what is and what is to take place hereafter (Rev. 1:9-19).

Second Vision (Revelation 4:1-16:21)

This vision is so long and has so many images and so much action that I must refer the reader to the Bible for the full account. I will list the characters and give a brief account here because of its significance in the sequence and series of visions.

The scene shifts from Patmos to Heaven. The place is the throne of God itself. The characters, in addition to the One on the throne and those worshiping Him, are the Lamb, the Woman, the Dragon, the Man Child, the Archangel Michael, the Beast from the Sea, the Beast from the Earth, and the Saints.

The following account is my paraphrase.

> A door is standing open in Heaven, and the first voice, like a trumpet, that I had heard speaking with me, said, "Come up here, and I will show you what must take place."
>
> Immediately I was under the Spirit's power, and I saw a throne in heaven with One seated on it. The One who was seated on it looked like jasper or sardius (carnelian) and around the throne there was a rainbow that looked like an emerald. Around the throne there were twenty-four thrones, and twenty-four elders seated on them, clothed in white and with crowns of gold on their heads.
>
> Out from the throne came flashes of lightning, rumblings, and peals of thunder, while in front of it seven flaming lamps were burning; they were the seven spirits of God. Also in front of the throne there was something like a sea of glass as clear as crystal. Around the throne, at the middle of each side were four living creatures dotted with eyes in front and behind. The first living creature was like a lion, the second was like an ox, the third had a face like a man's, and the fourth was like an eagle flying. And the

Visions of an Exiled Early Christian Leader

four living creatures have each of them six wings, and they are dotted with eyes all around and beneath the wings. And day and night they never cease saying:
"Holy, Holy, Holy is the Lord God, the Almighty, who was and is and is to come."

And whenever the living creatures offer glory, honor, and thanksgiving to Him who is seated on the throne, to Him who lives forever and ever, the twenty-four elders fall down before Him who is seated on the throne and worship Him who lives forever and ever, and they throw their crowns in front of the throne, and say:

"You are worthy, our Lord and God,
to have ascribed to you the glory, honor, and power;
For you created everything.
And since you willed it so, they came into existence
and were created."

The Lamb appears, who is introduced as the Lion of Judah whom we know as Jesus. Millions of angels, the four creatures, and the elders are worshiping Him. Then the voices of every creature in heaven, on earth, underneath the earth, and on the sea, and all that they contain are heard saying:

"Blessing, honor, glory, and power be to Him
who is seated on the throne
and to the Lamb forever."

The Lamb goes to the throne and takes a scroll, which is fastened with seven seals. The scroll is a book of history. The Lamb begins to unfasten the seals in silence with no cracking, no tearing, like melting the wax with the touch of an invisible ray of sunlight.[14] The scroll begins to open, revealing four horses, one after the other. They are white and red and black and pale gray and show all history, conquerors, war, famine, and terrible disease.

As the Lamb continues to break the seals in silence, the slaughtered faithful appear pleading with God for justice. "How long, O Lord," they cry, "before you stop the world and punish the wicked?" But still they praise God.

Finally, when the seventh seal is broken, all fury breaks out with confusion, chaos, and noise. There's an earthquake and heavy hail. Thunder rumbles. Lightning flashes. Trumpets sound. Mountains burn.

Part Three: Dreams and Visions in the New Testament

> Now John sees something that helps him to understand what is happening. He sees a woman clothed in the sun with the moon under her feet, and a crown of twelve stars on her head. She gives birth to the Male Child. Then a red dragon, with seven heads wearing crowns and ten horns lashing his long tail and breathing fire appears. The dragon tries to devour the newborn child. The woman flees. John sees a war breaking out in heaven.

Third Vision (Revelation 17:1-21:8)

This vision begins with the image of a woman dressed in purple and scarlet seated on a wild beast with seven heads and ten horns. The vision includes the final conflict of the war.

So far the story has unveiled why things are as they are, but now the story reveals the future and, finally, a happy ending.

A mysterious Rider on a white horse leading the "Celestial Calvary" appears. He is called Faithful and True. He wears many crowns on his head and a garment dipped in blood. His eyes are like coals of fire and a sword issues from his mouth. It is no ordinary sword of steel. It has been described as a sword of thought that could cut down the enemy, much "as a child blows on a feather to make it fly."[15] On the Rider's garment and his thigh is written, "King of kings and Lord of lords," so we know He is Jesus, who had been crucified under this sign. John sees the throne again and God seated on it making judgment. "Beasts, False Prophet, AntiChrist, Mammon, successive imperialisms, delusive techniques" all perish. All those perish, both kings and beggars, who throw themselves on their knees before even the appearance of Power.[16]

At last an angel shows John the outcome of the struggle: the New Heaven and the New Earth and a new beginning and peace.

Visions of an Exiled Early Christian Leader

Fourth Vision (Revelation 21:9-22:5)

John now sees the holy city coming down out of heaven from God, and he hears a loud voice from the throne say:

> See! God's dwelling place is with men, and He will live with them, and He will wipe every tear from their eyes. There will be no death any longer, no sorrow, no crying, no pain. The first order of things has passed away.

Then he who was seated on the throne says, "See! I am making everything new." The He identifies himself as the beginning and the end, who will, without cost, give to the thirsty water from the springs of living water.

Next John is taken by an angel to a great, high mountain and is shown the City of God, the New Jerusalem. While the angel talks with him, he measures the city with a measuring rod of gold, and the angel says he measures as man measures.

Because this New City is so splendid and lovely, John uses all the most dazzling, wonderful, precious things he can think of to describe it to his readers. He says it retains the glory of God and has luster like a precious stone, like jasper, clear as crystal. He can only tell us what it is like because he has never seen anything of this kind. He likens it to precious stones; gold, transparent as glass; pearls; perfect measurements; beautiful, clear light from the presence of God because there is no sun or moon and no night. It is a place were God is worshiped everywhere, so there is no temple or church. Nothing unclean can enter: no disease, no famine, no war, no death, no lying, no quarreling, no misery of any kind. A river of living water, clear as crystal, flows from the throne of God and of the Lamb through the center of the city. Trees of life line both sides of the river and they bear fruit continuously the year round. Moreover they bear twelve different kinds of fruit, and their leaves can be used for healing of the nations.

Part Three: Dreams and Visions in the New Testament

John says that when he saw and heard these things, he fell at the feet of the angel who was showing them to him, but the angel told him to be careful not to do this, that he is to worship God.

Jesus then speaks. "I, Jesus, sent my angel to bear this testimony to you for the churches. I belong to the line and family of David; I am the bright morning star."

And he invites all to come to everlasting life, saying: "Come. Let everyone who wishes come and take the living water without any cost."

The person seeing these visions is John, thought by many scholars to be John the Apostle, although there are some differences of opinion. For the purpose of this book, we'll consider him an early Christian leader. The Christians of Asia Minor were being persecuted for refusing to worship the Roman emperor's statue. John had been banished to Patmos.

The visions of John are called Revelation or the Apocalypse. We've already looked at two such apocalyptic accounts, Daniel's in the Hebrew Bible and Ezra's (II Esdras) in the Apocrypha, and now we read John's in the New Testament. All three reveal that an anointed delegate sent by God will redeem the Israelites and God's people and rule the world. *Messiah* is the Hebrew name for this "anointed one," and *Christ* is the Greek word for it. Christians believe Jesus, who was crucified, arose from death and was resurrected to be the anointed one. For this belief, they were persecuted and oppressed just as God's chosen people were in the Hebrew Bible. No doubt they were troubled about why God allowed the suffering of his people, just as the people of Israel were in the Hebrew Bible. John must have been pondering this very problem as he sat alone on the rocky little island of Patmos off the coast of Greece.

Some believe the use of the vision to be a literary device, and it may be. If so, the content still had to came from God in some extraordinary way, because John says that each vision came to him while it was he the Spirit. The visions are beyond human imagination. I have been on Patmos several times. One time it was just at sunset, and I could imagine John sitting there on

Visions of an Exiled Early Christian Leader

that rugged, rocky terrain, surrounded by sea water with rocks jutting out of its surface. The haze blurred and hid the line where the rocks and sea met, so that the tops of those rocks seemed to rise up out of the water and take on the shapes of monsters or beasts. In the sky streaked with color from the setting sun and cloud formations, I could see figures reminding me of God's angels and his heavenly court—the gulls and birds flying about the winged creatures. While I waited there for the bus to take me down to the harbor where I would take a tender to the ship, a strong wind came up and everything swirled about. I thought of the great Cosmic upheaval described in John's visions. At that moment I had no trouble believing that those images and his experiences could be used in visions to depict messages about issues that deeply concerned John, but the way they are put together is extraordinary.

John's response to his visions follow the requirement laid down by the prophets in the Hebrew Bible, which said that such experiences from the non-physical realm correctly understood would bring the viewer into closer relationship with God and not lead to the acceptance of false gods. Certainly John's devotion to the Living God is strengthened. He also uses his vision for the benefit of others and does not set himself up as privileged or more blessed than they. He understood this to be for others, and he wrote it down to comfort and encourage the persecuted of his time. It was a comfort not only to them but to people for all time.

The visions are in symbols that can be understood by the persecuted Christians but not by their persecutors. Much of the meaning has been lost to us; however, we still know the meaning of much of the imagery. For example, the Lamb always means Jesus. We know this by the way "Lamb" is used in this context and in other biblical writing, such as in John 1:28. Christians today understand the vision as a depiction of Jesus Christ as the redeemer with God in control and of the victory of the forces of good over the forces of evil. So these visions,

Part Three: Dreams and Visions in the New Testament

terrifying as they are in places, gave John assurance, gave the persecuted Christians in those times assurance, and can give us assurance.

If we wish to compare John's visions with our visions in our dreams, we find that as grand and unique as John's visions are, they are similar to our ordinary dreams. They use the language of pictures, and although they are out of the ordinary, we too can have out-of-the-ordinary images. Jung recognized this and arrived at the following conclusion for dealing with such imagery. Jung's words seem to apply to John's unusual symbols and images as well as our own.

> Whenever something turns up in a dream that has little or no connection with ordinary life...but where there are dragons or temples or something that does not exist in one's usual surrounding, then you can be sure that the unconscious is tending to convey the idea of something extra-ordinary, something uncommon, and it depends upon the nature of the symbolism to tell us what particular kind of extraordinary thing it is....[17]

John's visions deal with matters of deep concern and provide new information not only for the entire Christian community but also for him as an individual. It just might be that these writings are a record of John's inner spiritual journey, and the form of the images are a revelation of his inner spiritual life.[18]

The arrangement of the visions into a series deals with the same issue. We often dream in a series either during one night or over a longer period of time. In a series of dreams, single dreams group themselves around the same issue or problem. Each of John's visions has a different setting and sometimes the scene shifts within a single vision. This happens in our dream series, too. Each presents Jesus from a somewhat different aspect. People and things in our dreams are often also presented from different perspectives.

Reading these visions is an overwhelming experience, so I can appreciate what it must have meant for John to describe what he saw and experienced so that it could be understood with all of its magnificence by the suffering people to whom he was writing. Perhaps we would appreciate it more if we would put ourselves in John's situation and let ourselves see the whole panorama of strange events, characters, and places pass before our eyes. Or better yet, put ourselves in the persecuted early Christians' place and imagine reading it. What kind of feelings would we have? What meaning would it have for our lives? What would our response be?

Summary of Dreams and Visions in the New Testament

In the Hebrew Bible, it is primarily the favored class—the kings, nobility, priests, and prophets—who have the dreams recorded. In the New Testament, common people's dreams are also recorded: Joseph, the carpenter; Peter, a former fisherman who became a disciple of Jesus and had no official power or recognition; and Paul, who had given up any official position or status he may have had in order to be an apostle. There is a hint of the Hebrew Bible tradition in the wise men's dream (Matthew 2:12) and perhaps in Pilate's wife's dream (Matthew 27:19). The wise men were professional dream interpreters. Pilate was governor; however, a woman would not ordinarily have been considered a proper recipient of an official dream, and her dream certainly wasn't heeded by Pilate. Notice that both of these are warning dreams. The wise men were warned not to return to the wicked King Herod after their visit to the baby Jesus, but instead to return to their own country by another route. Pilate's wife's dream prompted her to warn her husband to "have nothing to do with that righteous man (Jesus), for I have suffered much over him today in a dream." He did not heed her dream, and Jesus was not protected.

Part Three: Dreams and Visions in the New Testament

Less imagery and symbolism is described in the New Testament dream reports, and there is no interpretation of dreams by a professional person.

As in most instances in the Hebrew Bible, the dreams have a large place in the dreamers' relocating geographically, but such a response is more pronounced in the New Testament. In fact, all except Pilate's wife's dream led to decisions regarding location.

The dreams in the New Testament are connected with the birth and nurturing of the baby Jesus, the Messiah foretold by the prophets of the Hebrew Bible; the further acknowledgment of the Messiah as a reality; and the spreading of his teachings. In other words, the dreams are focused on the Messiah, a person, rather than Israel, the Nation from which the Messiah came. Even Pilate's wife's dream dealt with protecting Jesus, the righteous man, although it failed due to lack of consideration.

The dreams continued to serve a purpose in the lives of the dreamers and provided assurance, comfort, alternatives, guidance, and instruction. They provided religious experiences that resulted in the development and growth of the dreamer as well as the founding and establishing of a religion.

That the dreamer benefits from the dream and the experience of dreaming is an exciting realization for me. God does not just use the dreams for His own purpose, as worthy as that may be in the long run; rather, He uses the dreams for everyone, including the dreamers.

Part Four
Dreams and Visions among Post-biblical Jews

Chapter 20

Dreams and Later Judaism

Dreams continued to be valued in later Judaism. We see this in Jewish literature of both mainstream Judaism and its branch of mysticism known as the Kabbalah. In their practices and understanding of the dreaming process, both point to observations of modern dream psychology.[1]

The Talmud is a written summary of Jewish oral law and is one of their documents of faith. It was compiled between the first and seventh centuries A.D. In its discussion of the interpretation of dreams, it states that an uninterpreted dream is like an unread letter. According to it, people continued to relate dreams to the spiritual realm and to God. Dreams were classified as good and bad; however, bad dreams were more transforming because they led the dreamer to repentance. This belief was a forerunner of our present-day belief that bad dreams address issues or attitudes that need attention. When the dreamer becomes aware of this and takes steps to resolve the difficulty, growth and healing occur in the dreamer's life. This is reflected in these words, found in an ancient Jewish prayer from the Talmud:

Part Four: Dreams and Visions among Post-Biblical Jews

> Sovereign of the Universe, I am thine and my dreams are thine....If they are good dreams, confirm and reinforce them....Turn all my dreams into something beneficial for me.[2]

The Zohar (The Book of Splendor) is the major writing of the Jewish mystics (the Kabbalah). It appeared in Spain in the thirteenth century. It is a commentary, composed during the time the Talmud was being finalized, on an early writing of the movement. It uses symbolic terms to describe the wonders of the universe. Its central image is the Tree of Life. The Tree of Life is the name given to the fundamental structure of energy within every living and inanimate object. Everything is in constant interplay, and its underlying order cannot be reduced or diminished. There is orderliness to everything, and "nothing that happens to us is viewed as meaningless or haphazard."[3]

In the teachings of Jewish mysticism, dreams and music are considered the two most direct and universal means of "recovering a full awareness of who we are as unique persons and what our purpose is on earth."[4] The Zohar and other writings of the Kabbalah recognize that our minds use symbols in our dreams, and these symbols represent thoughts and feelings that we may not be consciously aware of; thus, they may represent thoughts and feelings we are suppressing.

Divine prophesy is associated with dreams, and one source of extrasensory information is the dream, but according to the Kabbalistic tradition, "Discernment is a power to be more prized than exercising of extrasensory abilities."[5] While dreams can be a vehicle for clairvoyance and telepathy, psychic powers are not to be sought for their own sake.[6]

There is a slight distinction between dreams and visions made in the Zohar, which to my knowledge is not found elsewhere. In it a dream is described as "more precise than a vision and may explain a vision."[7]

The Jewish mystic understood that, during sleep, preoccupation with daily activities and concerns is shut off, and the sleeper becomes open to divine inspiration.[8] In other words, something we may have a closed mind to, either because of our attitude toward it or our inability to absorb it, can claim attention in our dreams while we sleep.

The reverence for dreams that we find in the Hebrew Bible and other early Jewish writings continued with Jewish philosophers such as Philo and Maimonides, stories of Hasidism as retold by Martin Buber, and the more recent book entitled *Rosenbaums of Zell*. This book about a rabbinic family portrays Jewish rabbis still paying attention to their dreams despite the Western world's lack of interest.[9]

About a year before reading these teachings of Jewish mysticism, I had the following complex dream, which contains some baffling imagery. I vaguely relate this dream as a whole to the inadequacy I felt while I was writing this book; the following images I relate to my ancient dream roots:

a jeweled tree
a goblet with ancient Hebrew letters
a water pump with a smiling face

The Missing Intercom and Mysterious Images

When I come into my house in the evening, I see that the intercom is missing along with a few treasured items I keep in the niches around it. I am frightened until I think that perhaps Dwight, my interior design consultant, is responsible. I go cautiously upstairs, and in the bedroom I find three women whom I know, although after waking I don't recall who they are. I think of them as friends.

Next morning I rush to get off to my teaching job. I'm panic-stricken because I'm going to be late. It's not clear how I get to school, but I suppose I drive because later I'm looking for my car.

I dash into the building and into my classroom a little late, and I see strange people all about. In my classroom I see a lot of women caring for infants on the desktops, and I think it looks like a child care center. I ask about my pupils and they know nothing about my class or where they had gone. I run out into the hall and look, but still don't find any of the pupils or regular school personnel. I am unable to find my way out of the school building. I go to one doorway and it isn't right. I go to the opposite side, look out, but see nothing I recognize. My car isn't parked there. I ask for help from some women who sit inside what looks like an information booth. They tell me how to leave the building.

Part Four: Dreams and Visions among Post-Biblical Jews

> Once I am outside, however, nothing looks familiar. I can't even find my way home. The people I run into do not speak so that I can understand. It gets really scary. I feel I need time to pull myself together, so I go into something like an outdoor market. It has a canopy held up by poles. Although it seems dark, my eyes having not yet adjusted from the bright sunlight to the shade, quaint items catch my eye. There's a tree with a splendid jewel- like bark and palm-like branches, a stemmed goblet decorated with middle eastern designs and the ancient Hebrew alphabet, and an old-fashioned water pump with a smiling face on the head of it opposite the handle. Suddenly I realize the ladies there are speaking in a language I understand, and I ask them, trying not to speak too fast in my panic and fear that their ability to speak English might disappear, how to get to where I live. They answer, but I don't understand what they say. When I open my mouth to speak to them again, a jingle in gibberish comes out. It would have been funny if I'd not been so astonished.

Now after reading the teachings and practices of the Jewish Mystics, I have learned that one ancient Jewish meditation centers on the letters of the Hebrew alphabet.[10] It is based on the belief that the alphabet carries sacred connotations. Its purpose is for the meditator to attain a deeper awareness of the divine through an altered state of consciousness. One of the variations is said to transport the practitioner from a whirl of typical thoughts "to a realm of dazzling peace and beauty."[11] The Hebrew letters on the goblet lead me to associate that part of my dream with these images of dazzling peace and beauty in the midst of swirling confusion. Truly my dream has spontaneously given me a gift of peace and beauty. I think of a goblet in a religious setting as a symbol of communion with God (i.e., the communion cup), though I can't put into words that feeling of being in communion with the Ultimate Source. This drinking vessel with Hebrew letters holds deep meaning, which no doubt fits into the total picture with the other two images and may offer more meaning together with them.

My dream tree is so grand and divine that I associate it with the Tree of Life named in Genesis and in Revelation. Trees are common motifs in dreams and visions. Nebuchadnezzar's dream tree and Moses' burning bush are instances of it in the Bible. In my dream, the tree by the water pump suggests to me the biblical verses, "He (the person who trusts God) shall be like a tree planted by the waterside (Jeremiah 17:8)" and "He (the righteous person) is like a tree planted beside a watercourse (Psalm 1:3)." I have dreamed of many different kinds of trees: transplanted trees, dying trees, a wintertime tree, a budding tree, an evergreen tree, a tree as a houseplant growing in water, trees by a stream. I feel they deal with different areas of growth in my life, and the trees beside the water in the Scriptures also seem to describe growth. Most trees in Palestine are dwarfed because of a lack of moisture, so a tree beside water is a symbol of the fullness of life. But my dream tree symbolizes more. Its jeweled, palm-like branches and straight trunk catch the fire even in the shaded light. It is so extravagant and so mysterious—and so still. Not that it can't move, but this seems to be a time for stillness. My jeweled tree can only be described as divine. The following vivid description in the Zohar immediately brought my tree to mind:

> From the midst of it (the House of the World at the center of the Universe) rises a large tree, with mighty branches and abundance of fruit providing food for all, which rears itself to the clouds of heaven and is lost to view between three rocks, from which it emerges, so that it is both above and below them. From this tree the house is watered. In this house are stored many precious and undiscovered treasures.[12]

My tree is not so giant, but it is as grand and as powerful an image. Can it be that my jeweled dream tree symbolizes God? The very thought is too awesome. I feel more comfortable thinking that because it is beside the water pump it stands for a fuller, more meaningful life.

And what of the pump with the smiling face? Why did my dream use such a strange image? A cistern would go better with the other ancient symbols. However, the water pump was something from my childhood, and as a child I pictured the wells in Bible stories as looking like our pump, although a pump is different. It is used for drawing water from way down deep in the earth, suggesting the depth of all I am experiencing in this dream. I remember the cool water drawn up by pumping the handle by hand, usually my

Part Four: Dreams and Visions among Post-Biblical Jews

mother's hand, and seeing the water run from the pump's spout. That the water was down in the earth and didn't get muddy and could be brought up to the surface to quench your thirst was a mystery to a child. And I think of a hymn in our church hymnal that begins "Spirit of God in the clear running water...." Clearly the pump has something to do with the deep mysteries of life; however the face is another matter. After considerable thought and many days, the term "well-pleasing" caught my attention and I had to laugh because I thought of my water pump with the smiling face. Of course, it was a play on words so common to dreams. This pump, which goes together with the tree and the drinking vessel, is saying something of its own. The pump with the smiling face gives to me its own blessing of "well-pleasing." I do not know what to make of all of this. Perhaps it is as Ingmar Bergman, the movie scriptwriter and producer, says.

> The dream is never intellectual....But when you have dreamt, it can start your intellect. It can start you intellectually. It can give you new thoughts. It can give you a new way of thinking, of feeling....It can give you new light for your inner landscape. And it can give you suddenly a little bit of a new way of handling you life.[13]

As if the mysteries so far in my dream were not enough, I lastly find myself speaking a jingle in gibberish. Could this be similar to the ecstatic utterances referred to as speaking in tongues? At first I thought the dream was telling me that this book about dreams didn't make sense and that the whole idea was nonsense. Why are we always so quick to take a negative view for the meaning of a dream? It was Morton Kelsey who asked if I had considered the possibility of receiving the fit of tongue-speaking through this dream. Speaking in ecstasy is a rare experience in Scripture, a gift one does not seek. I had not given it any thought, nor would I have regarded it a normative spiritual experience for me, yet in the context of the dream it makes sense. The dream's purpose is for communion with God. The communion cup, the meditation images, the "well-pleasing" of the spirit of God in the running water

Dreams and Later Judaism

are all brought together in ecstatic speech. My dream provided me with the experience of communion on a deep level with the Ultimate Source of all that is.

Actually none of these images are out of the ordinary. Trees, pumps, goblets, jewels, smiling faces, and even Hebrew letters are all part of my experience. It's the way they all come together that causes them to take on special meaning and meanings. They simultaneously carry me backward to my ancient roots and forward as this experience becomes part of my everyday life and as further meanings became apparent.

Chapter 21

Visitational Dreams among Moroccan Jews in Israel

Two university lecturers include the following dreams in their article on visitational dreams among Moroccan Jews in Israel. Visitational dreams are those dreams in which God or a supernatural power makes an appearance in order to encourage, comfort, or aid the dreamer. The dream visitor may also test or afflict the dreamer as a punishment. The article indicates how the Jewish folk religion as well as psychologists and sociologists value the place dreams hold in the therapeutic process.[14]

AN ENCOUNTER BETWEEN A SAINT AND A WOMAN DEVOTEE

The *saddig* came to me in a dream dressed in white and in his hands were mint leaves. He came near to the house and said, "Shalom, Arise! Arise!" in an authoritative voice. I cried and said

Part Four: Dreams and Visions among Post-Biblical Jews

to him, "How can I get up? I have headaches, tears from my eyes for over two months, from so much crying. No one helps me. Not the doctor. Nobody." He said to me, "Get up. Enough! You came to me, (to my tomb) and cried so much, I came to help you. Get up." He gave me his hand and raised me up. On the next day, the pains were gone, thank God. There certainly is a God and also saints in the world. He said to me, "Arise! Enough! You have cried so much, it hurts my heart."

Mint leaves are a traditional Moroccan symbol for blessing, fertility, and good health.

A YOUNG SOLDIER DREAMS OF DIVINE PROTECTION

Yesterday I dreamt that lions were chasing me and I cried out for help. In the morning, as I woke up, I asked my father to explicate my dream and he told me that "the Holy Lion," (the *saddig*, Rabbi Shimeon), pursues me and helps wherever I go.

The Holy One appearing in these two dreams is the saint (*saddig*). These saints refer to individuals who were believed to possess a special spiritual force that continues after death to benefit his devotees. Devotees show their deep interest and reverence for the saint by making pilgrimages to his tomb. One of these saints is Rabbi Shimeon, alleged author of the Zohar.

The purpose of the article is to show how personal concerns of the dreamers are cared for through the idiom of the saint, but I am interested in finding evidence of a continuity with the dream practices of the ancient Hebrews.

The dreams of the Moroccan Jews reflect personal life problems of women, some men, and even children, instead of being primarily revelations of the Deity to kings, priests, and prophets; however, they do feature many similarities to biblical dreams. In both we find the Holy One usually taking the initiative by sending a dream or speaking to humans in the dream. While the dreams of the Moroccan Jews are akin to the

Visitational Dreams among Moroccan Jews in Israel

incubational dream in that they are healing dreams and often occur at sacred places, they differ in that instead of the dreamer seeking a dream, the divine being appears without action on the part of the dreamer. The pilgrims, who visit the tomb of a saint, are not necessarily seeking a dream. Their pilgrimages consist of displaying pious behavior, bringing candles, oil, and food in exchange for the saint's looking after them. Two well-known biblical examples of people receiving dreams in a special place in which God takes the initiative are those of Jacob and the child Samuel.

Another similar feature between Moroccan and biblical dreams is that of the divine being appearing in the dream and identifying himself to the dreamer. Examples of the Deity identifying himself in the scriptures are Jacob's dreams in which the divine says, "I am the Lord, God of your father Abraham and God of Isaac" (Genesis 28:13) and "Jacob,...I am God, the God of your father" (Genesis 46:3). Another example is Moses' dream, in which he sees the burning bush and hears a voice saying, "I am God of your forefathers, the God of Abraham, the God of Isaac, the God of Jacob" (Exodus 3:6).

The following is from the dream of a middle-aged Moroccan Jewish woman.

> At night, I dreamt of someone, like a doctor, like a saint, all white, coming to me. I didn't recognize him. He said, "Do you recognize me?" I said, "No." He said, "They call me Nissim." It was the week of Hanukah, and the husband of my daughter is called Nissim. So I told him this, and then I woke up.

The doctor/saint in this dream identified himself with the name Nissim, which literally means "miracles" and is associated with saints. The time of Hanukah, the Festival of Lights, commemorates a time of miracles in Jewish history and further supports the identification of the saint. The dreamer acknowledges in the dream that she understands that he is a saint when she tells him her son-in-law is names Nissim. People are often named for saints and she is saying, "Yes, I know you are a *saddig* because my daughter's husband is named for you."

Part Four: Dreams and Visions among Post-Biblical Jews

There is a further connection in the dream with the saint in that both the Festival and the honoring of saints include the ritual of lighting candles.

In neither of these visitational dreams nor the scriptural dreams are the services of a professional interpreter required. The dreamers understand their own dreams upon awakening; in the case of the disguised saint in the visitational dream of the Moroccan, a family member may have been consulted. This can be observed in the second dream at the beginning of this chapter.

The ongoing relationship of the devotee and the saint is promoted by the visitational dreams of the Moroccan Jews. The relationship of the dreamer with God is enhanced through dreams in the scriptures when the dream is properly understood according to the prophets.

Both the ancient Hebrew dreamers and today's Moroccan Jews view their dreams as part of the sequence of events in their waking lives, as bridges between their pasts and their expected future outcomes.

While these dreams are not revelations of destiny for the individual dreamers or their people, they do appear to have many features of those recorded in Scripture.

Part Five
Dreams and Visions in the Early Church

Chapter 22

Dreams Prepare Early Christian Protesters for Martyrdom

PERPETUA'S DREAM VISIONS

There was a bronze ladder of extraordinary height reaching up to heaven, but it was so narrow that only one person could ascend at a time. Every conceivable kind of iron weapon was attached to the sides of the ladder: swords, lances, hooks, and daggers. If anyone climbed up carelessly or without looking upward, he/she would be mangled as the flesh adhered to the weapons. Crouching directly beneath the ladder was a monstrous dragon who threatened those climbing up and tried to frighten them from ascent.

Saturus went up first. Because of his concern for us [his pupils], he had given himself up voluntarily after we had been arrested. He had been our source of strength but was not with us at the time of the arrest.) When he reached the top of the ladder, he turned to me and said, "Perpetua, I'm waiting for you, but be careful not to be bitten by the dragon." I told him that in the name of Jesus Christ the dragon could not harm me. At this the dragon slowly lowered its head as though afraid of me. Using its head as the first step, I began my ascent.

Part Five: Dreams and Visions in the Early Church

> At the summit I saw an immense garden, in the center of which sat a tall, gray-haired man dressed like a shepherd, milking sheep. Standing around him were several thousand white-robed people. As he raised his head he noticed me and said, "Welcome, my child." Then he beckoned me to approach and gave me a small morsel of the cheese he was making. I accepted it with cupped hands and ate it. When all those surrounding us said "Amen," I awoke, still tasting the sweet cheese.
>
> I immediately told my brother about the vision, and we both realized that we were to experience the suffering of martyrdom; from then on we gave up having any hope in this world.[1]

Dreamer: Perpetua
Source: Her own written account of her arrest, imprisonment, and sentencing to the arena of the wild animals.

Perpetua was arrested and imprisoned in Carthage in 202-3 C.E. because she refused to offer sacrifices for the emperors' welfare. To do so would be in conflict with her Christian beliefs, and this was the way that she and others chose to "protest against those restrictions of state, society, and family which appear destructive of basic human freedom."

Perpetua was a twenty-year-old woman with a nursing child. She was of "good family and upbringing" and, according to her writing, was favored even above her brothers. Her family, except for her father, was Christian. At the time of her arrest, she was receiving instruction in the basic beliefs and teachings of the Christian faith. She was baptized after her arrest but before she was imprisoned, where she awaited death in the arena of wild beasts.

Prison was a terrible ordeal because of the darkness, the heat, and the milling crowd; however, the great part of her suffering was the anxiety and concern for those who were suffering because of her stand, especially her pagan father and her infant son. Her brother suggested that she ask for a vision indicating whether she would be condemned or freed, which she did. She felt confidence in speaking to the Lord because of the great favors he had already

Dreams Prepare Early Christian Protesters for Martyrdom

given her. She sought a dream for a certain purpose, which we call incubation: praying for a dream that will reveal the outcome of a particular situation.

The above is the dream she reported to her brother when she woke up the next day. She called it a vision. Because she was apparently asleep at the time of this vision, we call it a dream. Like her Hebrew Bible forefathers, she seems to make no distinction between a waking vision and a dream. The meaning of the dream was obvious to her: the outcome of the choice she had made would be martyrdom.

After a while she was granted the privilege of having her baby with her until a few days before her martyrdom. She accepted her martyrdom with courage, even anticipation. Her grief was for her father because he loved her so much and could not understand that she was responding to a duty greater than that expected of her as a daughter. He kissed her hands and cried, and she tried to comfort him. He suffered not only the emotional pain from what he perceived as rejection from a daughter he loved so much, but he also suffered physical abuse when he was thrown to the ground and beaten with a rod for interfering when she was brought before the governor to be questioned. When the governor asked, "Are you Christian?" he tried to persuade her to change her answer as she answered, "I am a Christian." On his last visit to her, he plucked out his beard and threw it on the ground, fell face down before her, and cursed his old age.

Perpetua dreamed once more before facing her martyrdom.

> The day before the battle in the arena, in a vision I saw Pomponius the deacon coming to the prison door and knocking very loudly. I went to open the gate for him. He was dressed in a loosely fitting white robe, wearing richly decorated sandals. He said to me, "Perpetua, come. We're waiting for you!" He took my hand and we began to walk over extremely rocky and winding paths. When we finally arrived short of breath, at the arena, he led me to the center saying "Don't be frightened! I'll be here to help you." He left me and I stared out over a huge crowd which watched me with apprehension. Because I knew that I had to fight with the beasts, I wondered why they hadn't yet been turned loose in the arena. Coming towards me was some type of Egyptian, horrible to look at, accompanied by fighters who were to help

Part Five: Dreams and Visions in the Early Church

defeat me. Some handsome young men came forward to help and encourage me. I was stripped of my clothing, and suddenly I was a man. My assistants began to rub me with oil as was the custom before a contest, while the Egyptian was on the opposite side rolling in the sand. Then a certain man appeared, so tall that he towered above the amphitheater. He wore a loose purple robe with two parallel stripes across the chest; his sandals were richly decorated with gold and silver. He carried a rod like that of an athletic trainer, and a green branch on which were golden apples. He motioned for silence and said, "If this Egyptian wins, he will kill her with the sword; but if she wins, she will receive this branch." Then he withdrew.

We both stepped forward and began to fight with our fists. My opponent kept trying to grab my feet but I repeatedly kicked his face with my heels. I felt myself being lifted up into the air and began to strike at him as one who was no longer earth-bound. But when I saw that we were wasting time, I put my two hands together, linked my fingers, and put his head between them. As he fell on his face I stepped on his head. Then the people began to shout and my assistants started singing victory songs. I walked up to the trainer and accepted the branch. He kissed me and said, "Peace be with you, my daughter." And I triumphantly headed toward the Sanavivarian Gate (Gate of Life). The I woke up realizing that I would be contending not with wild animals but with the devil himself. I have recorded the events which occurred up to the day before the final contest. Let anyone who wishes to record the events of the contest itself, do so.

This is the last dream Perpetua recorded in her prison diary. It previewed what she could expect as a combatant in the arena with the animals in front of the crowd, who would come to be entertained and to celebrate the emperor's birthday. It, also, provided her with the information that she would really be in contest with the devil himself rather than the beasts whose form the adversary would take.

This dream pictures Perpetua—mother, sister, daughter, and lady—as a skilled warrior. We see a gentle, motherly person exhibit the masculine characteristics (according to her culture) of boldness and directness. She is strong, fierce, daring, and courageous. The dream accomplishes this transformation by actually changing her into a man. This may be the dream's way of protecting Perpetua's modesty, since women were not ordinarily required to be participants in these public games, as well as of

Dreams Prepare Early Christian Protesters for Martyrdom

showing her she had the qualities within for handling herself in this order. The resulting image is of a universal Christian with both feminine and masculine qualities, indicating both are needed in the struggle against Evil. However, this does not detract from her identity as a woman, for it is as a woman (daughter) that she is awarded the victory branch by the trainer in her dream. Women seem to be considered equal with men when it comes to martyrdom. It is only within the church's hierarchal structure where they are not. We will see this reflected in the next dream, which is Saturus'.

I see in Perpetua's dream the dream's effort to integrate all the characteristics common to human beings, both feminine and masculine, into a well-balanced personality and character able to meet the demands of life.

Dreams today function the same way sometimes. Just this week, I was told the following dream which deals with the same issue:

> I see a man waist-deep in water. I go to him, and he holds me on his shoulder, pats me, and says "You know I've always loved you."

The dreamer said the dream made her feel accepted and good; she did not think of it as sexual. Still, she couldn't understand it. It was not a man she knew, so I asked her if he could represent masculine qualities or what she thought of as masculine qualities. Then I asked if "waist-deep in water" could mean "deep water," as in trouble. Or could it signify her half-hidden, masculine qualities, which lay deep in her unconscious but which sought recognition? If she recognized these qualities and turned to them, they might in turn help her accept her feminine qualities. Quickly she understood the man in her dreams to be a part of herself. Her dream was showing her that if she accepted these partially buried traits, they would enhance her womanly qualities and help her in her present circumstances.

Part Five: Dreams and Visions in the Early Church

SATURUS' DREAM VISION

Our suffering had ended (he said), and we were being carried toward the east by four angels whose hands never touched us. And we floated upward, not in a supine position, but as though we were climbing a gentle slope. As we left the earth's atmosphere, we saw a brilliant light, and I said to Perpetua, who was at my side, "This is what the Lord promised us. We have received his promise."

And while we were being carried along by those four angels, we saw a large, open space like a splendid garden landscaped with rose trees and every variety of flower. The trees were as tall as cypresses whose leaves rustled gently and incessantly. And there in that garden-sanctuary were four other angels, and more dazzling than the rest. And when they saw us they showed us honor, saying to the other angels in admiration, "Here they are! They have arrived."

And those four angels who were carrying us began trembling in awe and set us down. And we walked through a violet-strewn field where we met Jocundus, Saturninus, and Artaxius, who were burned alive in that same persecution, and Quintus, also a martyr, who had died in prison. We were asking them where they had been when the other angels said to us, "First, come this way. Go in and greet the Lord."

We went up to a place where the walls seemed constructed of light. At the entrance of the place stood four angels who put white robes on those who entered. We went in and heard a unified voice chanting endlessly, "Holy, holy, holy." We saw a white-haired man sitting there who, in spite of his snowy white hair, had the features of a young man. His feet were not visible. On his right and left were four elderly gentlemen and behind them stood many more. As we entered we stood in amazement before the throne. Four angels supported us as we went to kiss the aged man, and he gently stroked our faces with his hands. The other elderly men said to us, "Stand up." We rose and gave the kiss of peace. Then they told us to enjoy ourselves. I said to Perpetua, "You have your wish." She answered, "Thank God, for although I was happy on earth, I am much happier here right now."

Then he went out, and before the gates we saw Optatus, the bishop, on the right and Aspasius, the priest and teacher, on the left, both looking sad as they stood there separated from each other. They knelt before us saying, "Make peace between us, for you've gone away and left us this way." But we said to them, "Aren't you our spiritual father, and our teacher? Why are you kneeling before us?" We were deeply touched and we embraced them. And Perpetua began to speak to them in Greek and we invited them into the garden beneath a rose tree. While we were talking with them, the angels said to them, "Let them refresh themselves, and if you have any dissensions among you, forgive one

Dreams Prepare Early Christian Protesters for Martyrdom

another." This disturbed both of them and the angels said to Optatus, "Correct your people, who flock to you as though returning from the games, fighting about the different teams." It seemed to us that they wanted to close the gates, and there we began to recognize many of our friends, among whom were martyrs. We were all sustained by an indescribable fragrance, which completely satisfied us. Then in my joy, I awoke.

Dreamer: Saturus
Source: Written by his own hand for Perpetua's account of the days before their martyrdom

Saturus was probably an instructor in the basic beliefs and teachings of the Christian faith given to new converts before their baptism and therefore was Perpetua's teacher. It was appropriate that her teacher appeared in her dream as going up the narrow, dangerous ladder first so as to direct her in her ascent. Perpetua wrote that he was a source of strength. He had not been with his pupils at the time of their arrest, but because of his concern for them, he gave himself up voluntarily later.

He continued as a source of strength and an example to his pupils throughout their imprisonment and throughout the order of the arena. An eyewitness, possibly Tertullian, who wrote the introduction and conclusion to Perpetua's prison dairy, described Saturus' behavior going into the arena as well as his performance in the arena. He and those with him were scourged for informing the governor with gestures that as he was condemning them, God was condemning him.

Saturus had already decided he would die by one bite from a leopard, and that was the way it happened. He was first mauled by a bear, dragged by a wild boar, then tied to a bridge in front of a bear who refused to attack him. Finally, at the end of the contest, a leopard was set loose. Saturus went back into the arena, was bitten at once, and bled so profusely he collapsed. He died, fulfilling Perpetua's dream that he would be the first to climb the ladder and be her encouragement.

His dream gave him assurance of how it would be after their suffering ended, and that it would be worth it.

Part Five: Dreams and Visions in the Early Church

The dream with the bishop and priest standing outside the gate of heaven in disagreement concluded with Saturus and Perpetua approaching the gate. The clerics ask Perpetua, a laywoman, to help bring about a reconciliation between them. This opposed the practice of the church wherein an individual's importance was based on position rather than merit. She herself recognized their superiority and wonders about their asking her help. Not only was she a layperson, she was a woman. The angels interrupt, tell them to forgive each other, and remind them that their job is to correct their people who are fighting. The dream is telling Saturus that any person, a woman as well as a man, can approach God to effect their salvation. A person does not need to rely on clergy, who have other responsibilities.

Although the dream's main purpose is to encourage and reassure Saturus as to the outcome of the direction he has taken with his life, it deals with other issues. It is astonishing that dreams of such grandeur and so great a purpose can also deal with earthly problems.

Origen, an early churchman, expressed in his writings that he understood that dreams were not only for the benefit of the one who had the dream, but also for those who hear the account of it.[2] The author of the conclusion to Perpetua's account of her experience agrees when he calls these events, with their dreams, "sources of encouragement for the Christian Community." And so it was for some time. The account was circulated in both Latin and Greek. It was even used as part of the official church services. A basilica at Carthage was dedicated to her memory, and the anniversary of her martyrdom appeared in the official calendar of the Church of Rome. Augustine preached several sermons in her honor on anniversaries of her death, and her name was inserted in the Canon of the Mass of the Latin Christian Church.

These dreams continue to inspire, instruct, and encourage. Reading them and the circumstances in which they were dreamed reminds me of a quote from Synesius: "Dreams, more than any other thing, entice us toward hope. And when our heart spontaneously presents hope to us, as happens in our sleeping state, then we have in the promise of our dreams a pledge from the divinity."[3]

Chapter 23

Dreams among Early Church Leaders

After the death of the apostles and others who had known Jesus during his lifetime on earth, early Christians continued to value dreams as one way they related to God. The role of dreams in the personal lives of Christian theologians, bishops, preachers, and teachers—all well educated—is ecxititng and considerable. Their writings helped define what Christians believed.

Because of my lack of knowledge and experience with this material, I must rely on others' knowledge.[4] I will mention some of the dreamers and their views of dreams, with the hope that such brief treatment will not contradict my appreciation for them.

Part Five: Dreams and Visions in the Early Church

JEROME: A BIBLE TRANSLATOR DREAMS

The following was dreamed by Jerome, and he relates it in a letter:

> Suddenly, I was caught up in the Spirit and dragged before the Judgment Seat. The light was so bright there, and those standing around the Seat were so radiant, that I threw myself to the ground and dared not to look up.
>
> A voice asked me who and what I was.
>
> "I am a Christian," I replied.
>
> "You are lying," said the Judge. "You are a follower of Cicero, not of Christ. For where your treasure is, there also is your heart."
>
> Instantly, I became dumb. He ordered me to be scourged and, along with the strokes of the lash, I was tortured more harshly by the fire of conscience....
>
> I began to cry and wail, "Have mercy on me, O lord, have mercy on me." My cry could be heard amid the sound of the lash. At last, the bystanders fell down at the knees of the Judge and asked him to have pity on my youth, and give me a chance to repent. The Judge might still inflict torture on me, they insisted, should I ever again read the works of pagans....
>
> Accordingly, I swore an oath calling upon God's name: "Lord, if ever again I possess worldly books, or if ever again I read such, I have denied you!"
>
> On taking this oath I was dismissed.[5]

Jerome goes on to tell in his letter how when he awoke his eyes were drenched with tears, and he felt the bruises long afterwards. After that he wrote, "I read the books of God with more zeal than I had been giving to the books of men."

Jerome's response was one of intense emotion followed by action, which led Jerome to place his biblical studies above his studies of the classics. This eventually resulted in his translation of the Bible into Latin, which was the language spoken by the people in the Roman Empire then. This Latin translation was called the Vulgate.

Jerome was well versed in Hebrew and Greek, and he discussed the biblical dreams in his writings. We find that he valued dreams and visions and made no distinction between them. He agreed with Jeremiah that dreams can be used along with prophesying to turn people toward God. Like Jeremiah, he urged that care be taken in interpreting dreams and warned against using dreams for selfish reasons. He thought that those who understood the work of the Lord should explain dreams and wrote extensively about Daniel's dreams. He shared some of his other dreams, though some seemed to focus on him rather than directly on God and the furtherance of Christianity. These would fall more into the category of ordinary dreams, according to the dream system of the ancient Near East. This is characteristic of other dreams of this early church period, which signifies an acceptance of all dreams. He told one dream that sounds like exam anxiety dreams of contemporary students: he was a young man about to make a speech before his teacher and woke up relieved to find it wasn't so.

Why then, after all this positive experience with dreams, did he mistranslate a Hebrew word into Latin, causing dreamwork to be connected with witchcraft in such a way that dreamwork is condemned? He had translated this word correctly other times, so we know he knew the word. Neither do we find this condemning view of all use of dreams anywhere else in his works. Unfortunately, this was the beginning of the end of the Christian tradition of relating to God through dreams and visions in the Western world until recently.

TERTULLIAN

In the third century, Tertullian, whose father was a military man in North Africa, became a Christian while studying law in Rome. He wrote *A Treatise on the Soul,* which included eight chapters on sleep and dreams. This is the most authoritative discussion on dreams in the history of the Christian church, and in it he asks, "Is it not known to all people that the dream is the most usual way God reveals himself to men?"

Part Five: Dreams and Visions in the Early Church

Not only was he interested in dreams from the religious and spiritual viewpoint, scientifically he was ahead of his time. By watching children while they slept, he observed rapid eye movement, associated it with dreaming, and concluded that everyone dreams. (It was not until 1953 that we discovered this scientific fact with modern equipment.) He maintained that dreams were always meaningful and that a dream has various levels of meaning. He asks another question: "Now, who is such a stranger to human experiences as not sometimes to have perceived some truth in dreams?" He also warned against taking too much pride in considering ourselves especially blessed over others because of special dream experiences, suggesting "that we can hardly be crowned for martyrdom in our dreams anymore than we are condemned for visionary acts of sin."

ATHANASIUS

Athanasius of Alexandria lived in the fourth century. He was a courageous and brilliant man who was exiled three times for his struggle against heresy in the early church. His writings are authoritative for Protestant, Catholic, and Orthodox alike. He is credited for laying the foundation for all Christian thinking after his time. He showed from his earliest writing to his latest, a biography entitled *The Life of Antony*, that he understood dreams and visions to be revelations of an unseen world. Through his writing about Antony, we know of his belief that "the soul can be given direct communication with the nonphysical, the spiritual world" and that "dreams are one form of this communication."

SYNESIUS OF CYRENE

Synesius of Cyrene was a fifth-century, wealthy, North African man, well educated in "everything from geometry and astronomy to farming." He wrote a thoughtful, complex study of dreams that showed a great understanding of dreams for his time. He insisted that dreams could be understood only by checking them with outer experiences; dreams are personal and must be understood by the dreamer in terms of his/her own life. He felt that dreams should be recorded so that people would know their sleeping life as well as their waking one.

In his treatise *On Dreams,* Synesius expressed his belief that "the entire universe is a unity, and dreams express the meaning of the universe, including our relationship to it and to each other."

THE CAPPADOCIAN CHURCHMEN

There was a group of bishops of the Greek Orthodox Church during the last half of the fourth century who established the structure of the faith of the Eastern church. In their writing and speaking, they expressed conviction that God speaks through dream-vision experiences. It may be partially because of them that this conviction prevailed without interruption in the Eastern church to this day. Four of these bishops are Gregory of Nyssa and Basil the Great, who were brothers, Gregory of Nazianzen, and John Chrysostom. These men were well educated and from cultured Christian families. They were baptized into the Christian faith as adults.

Gregory of Nyssa helped to establish the Trinitarian thinking of the Eastern church. He wrote a book about the development of humanity, in which he dealt with the meaning of sleep and dreams. He believed that when a person is asleep, the physical senses and the sense of reason rest, and the less rational parts take over. Like Daniel and Joseph, he considered interpretation of dreams a gift form God. He saw daily occupa-

Part Five: Dreams and Visions in the Early Church

tions and events, the condition of the body, and the emotional condition of the personality all reflected in dreams. He told one of his own dreams in a sermon, entitled "In Praise of the Forty Martyrs," which honored soldiers persecuted for their Christian beliefs. In this dream these Christian soldiers, who had died in the freezing waters of a pond because they refused to deny their faith, lashed him with rods for his Christian lethargy. When he awoke, he was so shaken by his shallow devotion that he began to practice the Christian way more seriously.

Basil the Great believed that dreams were sources of revelation and referred in his writings to the Spirit's speaking to Jacob and Joseph through dreams. Basil's friend, Gregory of Nazianzen spoke at Basil's funeral, referring to Basil as a dreamer as great as Jacob and Joseph. A letter that he wrote to a woman who had sent him one of her dreams indicates that he interpreted dreams; however, in other writings he expresses concern over the misuse of dreams and warned about the gossipy nature of some interpreters. He also recognized the embarrassing nature of some dreams, and he had the bad experience of having dreams he had shared used against him.

Gregory of Nazianzen wrote of his dreams in theological poetry. His devotion to the Trinity was reinforced by his dreams.

John Chrysostom, a preacher in Constantinople, was such an effective speaker on every subject that he was called John the Golden-mouth. Because he practiced what he preached, he was banished twice by the Empress. He died near the end of the journey he was forced to make on foot the second time he was banished. He left no systematic treatment of dreams. However, writings about his studies indicate his effort to understand the dream experiences in the Bible, and in speaking he often discussed biblical dreams.

AUGUSTINE

Augustine (354-430 A.D.) was a Western theologian and one of the most intellectual people of his time. He had unusual psychological insights and was deeply religious. His writings contain references to dreams, visions, angels, and inner reality. He considered dreams an important means of understanding humankind and God, and believed they were given by God. Dreams—his mother's and his own—were significant in his religious pilgrimage.

Part Six
Dreams Today

Chapter 24

Our Ordinary Dreams and the Bible

Everynight dreams are ordinary dreams. People had them in Bible times just as we have them in our own times. Ordinary dreams—those that reflect the mental, physical, and spiritual state of the dreamer—are rarely reported in the writings of the Near East or in the Bible. This is because their focus on dreams differed from ours. Our interest in dreams centers on what dreams can tell us about our personal lives, while theirs centered on the religious and national or community causes. In the Hebrew Bible times, "the cause" was the establishing of a nation; in the New Testament, it was the establishing of the Messiah as the fulfillment of God's promises. Those that did not clearly fall into the religious and predictive classes were classified as pleasant or unpleasant according to the effect they had on the dreaming person. Those dreams were like our ordinary, everyday dreams.[1]

The pleasant, or good, dreams were probably those that "evoked pleasant emotions with an absence of the fear, the oppressiveness, and anxieties of the unpleasant. Apparently they saw no need to interpret and record these."

Part Six: Dreams Today

The unpleasant dreams were not told because of superstitious reasons. Maybe telling them might cause them to come true or at least give the dream more control over their lives. These were designated as "evil," "confused," "strange," "confounded," or simply "not good."[2]

This chapter first lists six dream effects—good and bad—common to both biblical and contemporary dreamers. This list is followed by a more in-depth discussion of these effects as caused by our dreams today.

EFFECTS OF DREAMS ON BIBLICAL AND CONTEMPORARY DREAMERS

1. Dreams frighten

"Thou dost scare me with dreams and affright me with visions (Job to God: Job 7:14)."

"In the anxious visions of the night when a man sinks into deepest sleep, terror seized me and shuddering; the trembling of my body frightened me" (Eliphaz to Job: Job 4:13-14).

"In dreams, in visions of the night,
When deepest sleep falls upon men,
while they sleep on their beds, God makes them listen
and his correction strikes them with terror"
(Elihu to Job: Job 33:15-16).

2. Dreams fade easily.

"He (the wicked) will fly away like a dream and be lost, driven off like a vision of the night" (Joseph to God: Job 20:8).

"...her (Jerusalem's) oppressors themselves fade as a dream, a vision of the night" (Isaiah 29:7-8).

Our Ordinary Dreams and the Bible

"...like images in sleep which are dismissed on waking" (Psalm 73:20b).

3. Dreams provide understanding about the nature of humankind.

"They (humankind) are like a dream at daybreak, they fade like grass which springs up in the morning but when evening comes is parched and withered" (Psalm 90:6).

"Human life is transient" (Psalm 90:6).

"In the anxious visions of the night...
an apparition loomed before me, and I heard,
'Can mortal man be more righteous than God...?'" (Job 4:13, 16-17).

4. Dreams instruct and help resolve problems.

"I set myself to think this out (why the wicked prosper and the righteous suffer), but I found it too hard for me, until I went into God's sacred courts (the Temple).
There I saw clearly what their end would be.
Then in a moment (I saw) how dreadful their end (the end of the wicked men who appear to prosper)...like a dream...dismissed in waking" (Psalm 73:16-17, 19-20).

We are not told that this writer was dreaming, but dreams are mentioned in connection with what he sees (Psalm 73:20). He may have gone to the Temple to seek a dream for help with a problem, which was then common practice. This visual experience showed him that the wicked in their prosperity would suffer the same outcome as a dream that is forgotten when the dreamer awakens. It reassured the writer that the righteous could expect to enjoy the constant counsel of God (Psalm 73:24).

Part Six: Dreams Today

This visual experience has another characteristic of a dream, when properly interpreted according to the teaching of the prophets: it brought the dreamer into closer fellowship with the one God. Ordinary dreams have this function as well as official dreams of prophets, priests, and kings.

> "My chief good is to be near thee, O God;
> I have chosen thee, Lord God, to be my refuge" (Psalm 73:28).

5. *Dreams can be pleasant like a wish that comes true.*

> "We were like (dreamers) who had found new health (whose wishes had come true.) (To the returning exiles, the new life of freedom first seemed like a dream [translator's footnote]" (Psalm 126:1 NEB).

6. *Dreams often speak of love and relationships and the pain of separation and searching.*

The following was dreamed by the first bride in Song of Songs 3:1-4:

> "Night after night on my bed
> I have sought my true love;
> I have sought him but not found him,
> I have called him but he has not answered.
> I said, 'I will rise and go the rounds of the city,
> through the streets and the square seeking my true love.'
> "The watchman, going the rounds of the city found me,
> and I asked, 'Have you seen my true love?'
> "Scarcely had I left them behind me when I met my true love.
> I seized him and would not let him go..."

The following was dreamed by the second bride in Song of Songs 5:2-8:

> I sleep but my heart is awake.
> Listen! My beloved is knocking:
> Bridegroom speaking in her dream:
> Open to me, my sister (term of endearment),

my dearest, my dove, my perfect one;
for my head is drenched with dew,
my locks with the moisture of night.
  I have stripped off my dress: must I put it on again?
I have washed my feet, must I soil them again?
When my beloved slipped his hand through the latch hole...
With my own hands I opened to my love,
but my love had turned away and gone by;
my heart sank when he turned his back,
I sought him but I did not find him.
I called him but he did not answer.
  If you find my beloved, will you not tell him
that I am faint with love?

DREAMS CONTINUE TO AFFECT US TODAY

Dreams Frighten

We've all experienced dreams that frighten us, just as they frightened Job and Job's friends. Dreams in which we find ourselves trapped, endangered, and unable to communicate or to protect ourselves are called **nightmares.** They reflect some unresolved conflict or situation. They may warn us that we need new understanding if our lives are to go well.[3] By "warning" dreams I don't mean "prophetic" dreams, which give data about the future and can be tested against the reality of later events. Rather, warning dreams are ones that help us see the outcome of certain behavior.

Recently I was told by a highly competitive person that in her dreams her friends were killed. These dreams occur at exam time or in some situation in which she wanted to excel. She was not satisfied to do well or better than she had previously. She wanted to excel over her classmates, especially her best friends. These

Part Six: Dreams Today

dreams did not predict the death of her friends, but warned her that she was alienating them because of her behavior. She was killing her friendships with her intensely competitive spirit.

Some dreams are scary because of a frightening dream figure or monster in them. I have learned that it is better to approach such a figure with the desire to understand it rather than avoid it. Converse with it as the biblical dreamers did with dream messengers. Ask them "What do you want?" or "What do you represent?" Doing so often results in the transformation of the attacking figure into a friendly one. "Loving the enemy" in your dreams may in fact turn out to be loving that part of yourself that you dislike, which the figure represents.[4] However, sometimes a figure that is not so frightening in appearance may exhibit challenging, testing, limiting, diminishing, or destroying behavior and, therefore, be very scary. I have a dream like that, which I call the "Evil Woman" dream.

> In this dream a woman took over my house. She even took over me. She told me what to do. She told me how to do it. She had me working for her in my own house. She was an attractive, middle-aged woman. She made out like she was nice and brought me things that looked on the outside like gifts. Once she gave me what appeared to be flowers wrapped in pretty paper. When I removed the paper, it turned out to be dead branches. Although she was pretty in a proper sort of way, her behavior was not pretty. She was thoughtless. She made work for me by strewing garbage about; once she ate an apple and just threw the core on the floor. I asked her to leave my house, and she laughed in such a way as to say, "What do you think you can do about it?"

When I awoke from this dream, I felt helpless and afraid and angry. In thinking over what was going on in my outer life just then, I realized there was a situation that may have called forth this dream and the strong feeling it left with me. I asked myself questions, "Who is this 'evil woman influence' in my life, who appears proper yet imposes her values and traditions on my life? Is there some part of me that demands that I follow someone else's rules?"

Our Ordinary Dreams and the Bible

The fact is, there is a part of me that is too accommodating, a part that is inclined to please people just to keep peace because I don't like confrontations or to seem different. I know that about myself already. Putting these two factors together, this dream reminded me that this "evil woman influence" comes to me both from within and without and tries to take control. This is not good for me. Nor is it good for those who depend on me for my special abilities. She challenges me with "What do you think you can do about it?"

After considerable reflection, the question came to my mind, "How would Jesus, who showed us God's love, apply God's love to this situation?" The answer: "Jesus said, 'Love your enemies,' but he didn't say, 'Let your enemies control you.'" Jesus never let his enemies control him, but neither did He avoid them. He knew in his wisdom that to avoid something or to run from something gives that something power over us. Instead of avoiding his enemies, He went ahead with what He believed to be his work of doing good, teaching and showing people what God's love was like. He did this according to whom he understood himself to be and not according to others' expectations of him. I might not be able to get rid of this "evil woman influence," but I do not have to let it push me around and control my life.

Recurrent nightmares may originate in traumatic circumstances such as war or abuse. Anger toward parents over one's treatment as a child, even though it might not have been abusive, is an area of unresolved conflict reflected in dreams. Although one may learn to express anger in non-destructive ways, it is not until one can view parents from a new, less personal perspective that true resolution happens. One may wish it had been different, but this new view brings forgiveness. "No longer is the issue 'something that shouldn't have happened in my life, something I didn't deserve,' but the wounds of the parents are somehow integrated into the destiny of the children."[5]

In dealing with nightmares, we are often able to bring healing to the circumstances that caused it. This may not happen at once, or once and for all. Healing takes time and is an ongoing process working toward wholeness (salvation). Dreams always promote

Part Six: Dreams Today

growth and healing. King Abimelech's experience with Abraham and Sarah is a clear biblical example of healing as the result of dealing with a dream. When he was told in his dream that he was as good as dead (Genesis 20:3f.), he set about correcting his mistake and "God healed Abimelech, his wife and his Slave girls..." (Genesis 20:17).

Dreams Fade

Most dreams are forgotten or soon fade upon awakening. Even those we recall and work with often vanish. My "Heavenly Blue Kitten" dream showed me this even before I realized the Bible refers to the fading of dreams. I'm constantly surprised with how many dreams deal at least partially with dreams. I don't think this one is just telling me that dreams fade, but that I need to give greater priority to them and to the inner life they symbolize.

> I'm leaving the house. I open the door to go out and downstairs to the car in the garage, and sitting there on my doorstep is this little kitten as blue as the sky. The color is the most startling, unnatural blue for a cat—not the grayish blue of blue cats. He almost glows. He sits looking up at me with golden eyes as bright as the early morning sun shining behind him. He has a look of such expectancy and trust that even if I had not already been fond of cats I could not have gone on. I take a little time to pet and feed it. It silently accepts my attention. Then I remember that I have some place to go, and I leave as planned. When I return that evening, my other cats show up, lazily stretching and yawning, from their secret sleeping places and acknowledge my return. But where is the little blue kitten? I look everywhere in the late afternoon shadows and do not find it. I'm afraid for it. I try to comfort myself with the idea that cats are well known for their homing instincts and maybe it went home. Still, it was only a kitten, too young to have developed this quality. I wake up sad and distressed.

It didn't require much work to figure out that what came to me in the form of a kitten in the morning was my dreams, and I became aware that the glowing blue kitten represented something of my spiritual or inner nature. And although I gave the kitten a little attention, it had gone by evening. If I had taken it more into

Our Ordinary Dreams and the Bible

my life that day, it might have stayed with me. Is this dream another way of telling me "seek first the kingdom of God and all the other things I need would be taken care of"? (Matthew 6:33).

Dreams Provide Understanding about Human Nature

Our ordinary dreams are mostly about ourselves and tell us things we may not want to acknowledge or have not recognized. They keep on telling us when we forget, too. I have had many humorous dreams that remind me to add a light touch to my life because I'm inclined to get caught up in drudgery or to feel burdened at times. The following three short dreams point out the different ways dreams can address an issue and how they can help you get things back into balance.

The first is entitled "Playful Ted."

> I am teaching school. It's lunchtime, and Ted comes into the lunchroom and sits at another table. He takes a knife and cuts three beautiful blossoms from the flowers in a vase on his table. He tosses them toward me like a playful schoolboy. This makes me giggle like a schoolgirl.

This dream called attention to my need for a more playful approach to my work—more of Ted's playful manner.

The second is entitled "My Sister's Christmas Gift."

> I open the package from my sister. It contains a green and white splashy print thing that at first reminds me of a small piece of luggage. As I take it out, it expands like an accordion folder. As I pull out the compartments, the flap unfolds into what looks like an apron top with ties. I put the thing on like it was an apron and fasten the strings around me. I laugh at seeing this big pouch with compartments stretch out before me.

This was a time of making a decision about moving. Thinking of all packing and organizing on top of Christmas activities and other things overwhelmed me. My dream had my fun-loving sister adding a light touch by putting the tools of my work together with

Part Six: Dreams Today

splashy, carefree green and white paint. I was reminded to take time for a picnic on the beach, or have a cup of tea on the porch while packing, or find something silly to laugh about.

The third dream is called "Julie and Jane."

> I'm visiting Julie and Jane at college. Julie's garment bag is laying on the bed. I unzip it and discover pockets on the inside for books, paper, and her school materials. Her school things are neatly organized in it. Although it looks like a piece of luggage, it's really a book satchel. I think this is really a great idea and so like Julie to be so organized. Jane comes bouncing in and dances and sings down the hall and out the dorm into the sunlight. She's wearing a cheerful pink and white checked dress. It's sleeveless and short just above her knees and looks so playful with red and white larger checked ruffles around the armholes, neckline, and hem. She's singing, "I'm off to Barcelona...."
>
> I think of my son, John, and wish he could be as organized with his schoolwork as Julie and as happy as Jane. I wonder how I can help him.

I wake up and think, "How can I help him in the state of confusion and dread I find myself in?" Then I realize that this dream is probably not so much about my son's needs as it is about mine. I need a way to deal with the confusion of moving and the dread of having to start all over in a new place. Not only that, but before I would have time to really adjust to a new place, my husband and I were supposed to go on his sabbatic leave, which would take us to Hong Kong, Singapore, Penang, Malaysia, and finally to live in Taiwan for four-and-a-half months. I felt I didn't have enough energy to even think about it.

Then I thought, "Where is the energy in this dream?" The part of the dream that was full of energy and all light and bubbly with dancing and singing must be the clue to dealing with my problem. Then two scriptures from the Bible reminded me to take one day at a time: "Rejoice for *this* is the day the Lord has made, *be glad*" (Psalm 118:24), and "Let today's own trouble be sufficient for today" (Matthew 6:24). The paraphrasing here came to me just this way to emphasize what I must do today and each day. This dream is asking me to approach my life with a more playful attitude. Notice this dream does not tell me what to do. It does, however, present me with another perspective.[6]

Our Ordinary Dreams and the Bible

Dreams sometimes show us something about ourselves through the other characters who appear in our dreams. They may represent aspects of ourselves or some quality we wish we had. Dreams capture the essence of such persons perfectly. I once dreamed of Jo, a young friend, who was hopping barefoot over rocky terrain while I picked my way slowly in my worn-out canvas shoes. In the dream I said to her laughingly, "Jo, you are just like a mountain goat." It wasn't until after her death when a teacher friend of hers wrote a memorial poem entitled "She Walked Easy on this Earth" that I realized how well my dream described her. This dream was not just about how gracefully she used her youthful body, it dealt with the skill of handling life.

Dreams Instruct and Solve Problems

Dreams as Instructors

Nearly all kinds of dreams have an element of instruction. Bible dreams often did. Such dreams usually will not give information or facts. They don't teach that way. Instead they give us actual experiences with a lot of feeling, which help us understand something new or another viewpoint. This happened to many Bible dreamers, from Abraham's first recorded dreams right on through Simon Peter's and the New Testament. In my experience these instructional dreams are not always so easy to understand (or accept?); however, this little jewel, which in fact uses jewelry in imagery, is pretty straightforward with me. It came at a time of transition in just about every way: I had moved; I was not going to continue my teaching career; I was feeling the physical pangs of the upper limits of middle age; I was moving from a more casual, carefree culture where women were more individual in their own right to a more traditional one where women my age were more of an extension of the husband's role in society. I hadn't yet found my own place, nor did I really know what I wanted. I call this dream "The Two Necklaces."

Part Six: Dreams Today

> An elegant woman appears. She's ageless, or timeless. She reminds me of the "Art Nouveau-an" fashions. She looks like a black and white fashion sketch, dressed in a sleeveless, flowing white dress of that time and her straight black hair is done loosely into a bouffant style. Even her skin is white. I've lost a gold necklace, which I'm looking for. It is of solid heavy gold wire and looks as though it's all one piece. Actually, one side coils around the other side in front and forms sort of a tassel on the end. The elegant woman offers me another gold necklace, a chain in links with gold coins dangling from all around it. I say it's lovely, but I really need to find this other one. I finally do and try to return the other one, but she says, "No, just keep it. You may want to use it, too, sometime."

At first I saw this dream as offering me a choice between two lifestyles. The first necklace reminds me of what a dignified African queen might wear—formal and more ridged—accommodating to her station in life. The second one reminds me of what an Egyptian dancer might wear—more casual and fun—abandoning everything in her own joyous activity. What I think my elegant dream friend is suggesting is that I might want to consider both ways of being. I might want to wear one sometimes and the other at other times or even experiment with combining them. It didn't have to be an "either or" choice. This dream gave me a third choice to think about.

Dreams as Problem Solvers

Problem solving is part of the nature of dreams, regardless of what other issues they deal with. Dreams make us aware of some information we already have within us but haven't considered in the light of a problem. Most of our dreams instruct us in daily personal living. There are also dreams that suggest the solution to specific problems. Gayle Delaney, in her book *Living Your Dreams,* presents several stories of dreams solving specific problems. One of these is about a young engineer at Bell Telephone Laboratories, D.B. Parkinson. In 1940 he was trying to solve a problem that would improve telephone technology. He had a dream that not only provided the answer to his problem but also led to the development of the M-9 electrical analog computer, making possible the first all-electric gun director. The latter development played a significant role in bringing World War II to an end.

Another dream more commonly known is one that led to the invention of the sewing machine by Elias Howe. The needle we use in hand sewing has the hole for threading in one end and the sharp point for pushing the thread through the cloth in the other end. Howe was puzzled about how to make the needle work in a machine when he had a dream in which he was being attacked by natives with spears. The spears had holes in the sharp, pointed end. He recognized this as the solution to his problem. The needle needed to have the hole in the pointed end to work in the machine.

There are many ways our lives are touched by the problem-solving dreams of the others. Thomas Edison believed that a number of his inventions came to him in the drowsing moments between periods of work; John Newton became a clergyman and a hymn-writer as the result of a dream; Coleridge, Wordsworth, and Robert Louis Stevenson are but three of many whose writings are based on dreams; Mahatma Gandhi gave the modern world the non-violent mass strike as a method of resistance due to a dream.

Our own dilemmas may be in areas of relationships, business decisions, career choices, and personal growth. Answers to these are not always so obvious. More often than not, our dreams present us with another way of looking at the situation.

Because dreams utilize resources we have already developed through past experience, we should not expect dreams to solve new problems if there is nothing relevant in our background from which to draw.[7] For example, a scientist would not likely get help with writing a music composition nor would a music composer get a suggestion leading to a new discovery in science. This doesn't mean a scientist might not dream about music or that science might not appear in a musician's dream. When they do, they probably represent something else.

I once had a beautiful dream in which a leafless, winter tree was covered with icicles hanging from all its branches. The icicles fall—first one, then two, then several, until many are falling, faster and faster. Each time one fell it made a note of music. This

Part Six: Dreams Today

continued until the music reached a crescendo. Then the icicles began to fall more slowly and fewer at a time, and the music followed the same pattern, until there was only one left—and it falls.

I entitled this dream "Winter Symphony," but I don't know music theory or how to write music. Nor was I learning music composition or theory. That, in addition to the rest of the dream, indicated that they stood for something else going on in my life. Each place where an icicle had been, a little bud appeared. This had a couple of meanings to me. After a "wintertime" in my life, there was warmth and the promise of spring time. The buds also depicted new growth and change taking place within. The music expressed my feeling of joy and wonderment. Since I'm almost totally without music ability, this expression was like a divine gift. This did not resolve any problems in a specific way in my life, but it did help me make a discovery about my personal growth and change.

Dreams Please

Dreams can be pleasant like a wish that comes true. Some such dreams have already been told in this book. Here is another.

The dreamer was engaged at the time, and her engagement was going so smoothly she couldn't believe it. She asked herself, "Can a relationship this happy last?" This dream, entitled "Dancing Redwoods," came as a response to her question.

> I saw a beautiful, sunny, redwood forest where two magnificent redwood trees were dancing in the wind. They were young, graceful, and majestic. I realized that the taller tree symbolized [my fiance] S., and the smaller beside it, myself. Then I was aware of our having become these trees. We were at peace with the world and would grow in the forest for centuries to come.[8]

Another dream is called "Wonderful Dream" by the dreamer, who had given up her baby for adoption. The baby was the result of a rape when she was sixteen. At the time of the dream, the baby would have grown to be twenty-five. She had wondered about this

Our Ordinary Dreams and the Bible

baby daughter and hoped she was happy all these years. No doubt this dream reflects her wishes for herself as well as for her daughter.

> In this dream she is traveling to Paris where she accidentally finds her long-lost daughter. Her daughter is about sixteen years old in the dream. They have a marvelous reunion, touring a number of cities together, and she entertains her daughter the way F. wished her mother had treated her. She is thrilled that her daughter so readily understands why she, F., had to give her up for adoption.[9]

If you would like your dreams to be more pleasant, you might suggest to yourself or request in prayer that you will not have unpleasant dreams, unless they are going to deal with situations you can do something about.

Some pleasant dreams I have had come from working happily on some satisfying project. Others come as a surprise, like a special gift, such as the one that follows:

> I awaken with a child singing "Heavenly Father, we adore Thee" in a beautiful, angelic voice. I am in a place where children are together—a summer camp-like, relaxed atmosphere. One child, a young boy about kindergarten age, is so delightful— childlike, but unspoiled. He is beautiful with dark, loose curls framing his face. Jessie and Penrose come up to me with pictures, saying, "We thought you would like to see these pictures of this child. They are so good." I look at them and agree that they are good and really show what a beautiful child he is. Next it is time to eat and without any announcement this child sings "Heavenly Father, we adore Thee," and everyone else joins in as a way of saying grace before the meal.

I awoke from the above dream on Father's Day morning. At first I entitled it "A Delightful Delighted Child." Now I call it "Joy" because it seems to depict pure joy and because of the events that followed. The previous day my husband had one of those rare days when he was not working or traveling, and we had gone to a town in Indiana where we had never been, just to explore. We saw an old home built by its founders, and we visited antique places and used bookstores. We bought a funny old popcorn popper for only three dollars, and some paperback books, and ate at a

Part Six: Dreams Today

cafeteria featuring country cooking. We had a pleasant time. In addition we were both happy because our son had just passed with distinction the comprehensive exams required as part of his Ph.D. program. The dream seemed to be an extension of a pleasant time and an expression of gratefulness for it. On the following Tuesday, I attended a seminary chapel service to hear our friend, Penrose, speak. His wife, Jessie, was there. Imagine my surprise when I found that we were singing "Praise the Lord! Ye Heavens, adore Him"—slightly different words but the music of my dream. Then Penrose spoke about "Joy" and presented a picture in words of "true joy." The dream seems to be one for enjoyment more than interpretation, and, perhaps, it also served to call attention to the significance of real joy and what it meant.

Dreams Speak of Love and Relationships

When it comes to dreams that speak of love, relationships, separation, and searching, much can be written. However, dreams can be private and often involve others, so I am reluctant to write about my own. I've had many beautiful dreams of this kind shared with me, but I feel I should treat them with the same consideration I give my own.

Relationships of all kinds are one of the most prominent themes dealt with in ordinary dreams. This includes simple friendship, business partners, parent/child, doctor/patient, and many others, as well as love and marriage relationships. Quite often, these relationships depict things going on inside of us.

I will share one of my dreams entitled "Looking into the Pool." The time of this dream is my thirty-third wedding anniversary. My husband and I decided we felt more rheumatic than romantic, so we went to Calistoga, California, for a weekend of the baths for which they are famous. This was a couple of weeks before we were to move from California to Kentucky. We had sorted things, had a garage sale, and taken care of business, so we were tired with

Our Ordinary Dreams and the Bible

aching joints. Along with the special baths and treatments, there was a swimming pool with a Jacuzzi to enjoy. The following dream is the dream I had on our anniversary night:

> I look into a pool of water and to my surprise I see two lions, a beautiful lioness and her mate, lying on the bottom of a pool of crystal clear water. I think they are dead, and I look away in shock. I look again and this time I see my cat and dog on the bottom of the pool. I think they have drowned and I am distressed. I bring myself to look again more carefully and see that they are really sleeping.

I was so puzzled by this dream that I shared it with the dream group with which I was working. Although it was a small dream, it took up most of the session. We explored what lions are like, how they live, and my experience with lions. Then with the question, "What do these sleeping lions remind you of in your own life?" we shifted to my cat and dog, because that is what the lions reminded me of. My dog has a fluff of fur around his neck that looks like a male lion's mane. He and my cat do sleep together, or near one another, frequently. Members of the group continued asking what my dog and cat were like and how they related. I answered that they do relate in an interesting way. They appear to be company for each other at times, missing one another when one is gone for some reason. They play and fight with one another. Other times the dog gets jealous of the attention I give the cat and will nose him off my lap. All in all, I would say they have a workable relationship with *some* understanding of each other.

But why are they in the bottom of the pool sleeping? I ponder this. The pool is crystal clear with hardly a ripple. It is peaceful, relaxing, and calming. It invites daydreaming—just the sort of setting for romance, but when I look into the pool I see sleeping lions and pets. The fact that I used *look* and *see* frequently in describing this dream was called to my attention by the group. Perhaps this crystal pool is a magnifying glass or a spotlight for focusing my attention on something. But just what is it that my dream wants me to see? Could it be that the pair of sleeping lions represents a peaceful, harmonious, and vital marital relationship?

Part Six: Dreams Today

Is it showing me what I consider the ideal, and then bringing me closer to home by showing me my pets? Is it saying, "Look at your dog and cat. This is what you are. The two of you are different, yet you manage to work things out."

The following dream was shared with me. In it, Arnold is separated from his wife after she argues with her friend. It deals with the inner dynamics of his personality. I call it "The Giant Dark Tower."

> I see this giant dark tower. It's black. It's made of big, black blocks of stone. It is very tall and has no windows. I think of it as impregnable, and there's a room right in the middle. I am in city streets that remind me of being in a European city. I am at the base of this giant, dark tower with Fielder. (Fielder and his wife, Anna, are friends of ours.) There has been a terrible happening. The feeling is like that connected to the Kent State University incident when the students were shot down during their protest. Lillian, my wife, and Anna are up there in that tower in chains being tortured. I am aghast and say, "We've got to go up there and free them." Fielder doesn't want to go, but he comes along. We are lurking around so we won't be seen. Somehow we wind up in the tower and get into the room where they are. There they are, and there is this person that looks like a Gestapo agent in black taking genuine pleasure in hurting them. It's a total shock to me.

This dream expresses separation in several ways. First, it reflects Lillian and Anna's terrible, real-life fight and subsequent broken friendship. This is the terrible happening.

Second, Arnold is separated from his wife, who is held prisoner by a torturer in a giant dark tower. The dream alerts him that this separation bothers him. It doesn't bother his friend, Fielder, so Fielder doesn't feel a need to do anything about it. (Fielder may also represent a part of Arnold that doesn't want to confront this danger.) In the dream, the anger Arnold held in all his life is torturing him and his wife.

The torturer's pleasure at hurting Lillian does not necessarily mean that Arnold takes pleasure in hurting her. He didn't understand this aspect of himself in the dream, but it was clear to him that this expression of anger between Lillian and Anna had stirred up the anger in him. He had never learned how to identify and

Our Ordinary Dreams and the Bible

admit to anger, much less how to express it. Now he was learning to do this, and the dream reported to him that he was beginning to take action by going inside (to the middle room) and facing it.

Separation, alienation, and isolation often show up in dreams, and they usually indicate something (not always anger) about our feelings and our inner lives.

Chapter 25

Our Extraordinary Dreams

> In the Dreamworld where the strange and unusual are commonplace, how can we introduce the topic of strange and unusual dreams? (Savary, *Dreams and Spiritual Growth*, 206).

Dreams which evoke wonder when we are told about them"[1] and have meaning for the listener as well as the dreamer and are not easily forgotten by either are often called uncommon or out of the ordinary. In this way they are like religious experiences. Some dreams might be called "elegant dreams."

A psychologist speaking on "the nature and characteristics of 'deep' dreams" acknowledged the specialness of some dreams. He says, "As we listen to individuals share their dreams we are occasionally struck by the richness of certain unusually poetic dreams." He refers to such dreams as elegant. He suggests that we accept such dreams as life motivating experiences and base our understanding of dreams on the dreams themselves and what they directly reveal.[2] This

Part Six: Dreams Today

reminds me of the practice followed by biblical dreamers. It is also what another psychologist, Henry Reed, whom I mentioned in the story of Jacob in the Hebrew Bible, says.

A friend, Josie, beautifully describes her special dreams: "They are like an opportunity to take another look—to have another view; these dreams are like the molding of me from the inside out. These dreams sculpt me. They are life dreams, without which I would be a very different person. The language is different. They continue to have a deep meaning—continue to surface and in some way are ever present—never really forgotten, *ever*."

In a book entitled *A Pilgrimage of Dreams*, the author of the introduction writes that the dreamer is aware that in some dreams there is life-giving meaning of a far deeper order than found in other dreams. A mark of these "great" dreams is that they are as meaningful to us as our own when we hear them or read them.[3] In her preface, the author, Thetis Blacker, says,

> Yet the dreams which I recorded here seem to come from a source which is not merely personal to me...on telling of them to a number of my friends, these dreams of mine have been recognized by other people as significant to them also, and relevant to their lives....For me they seem to be kind of pilgrimage, and from them I have learned much of the meaning of my life....these dreams seem to me to have come by Grace. The quality and atmosphere of them is totally different from the usual jumbled meandering dreams which I experience most of the time in my paradoxical sleep....They possess a clarity, a coherence, a vividness, a translucence, and a significance never found in ordinary dreams of every night....these dreams seem to have come to me from some place deeper than my ordinary ego...beyond myself...usual barrier of consciousness, within and without, have for those moments of sleep or wake been penetrated, or dissolved.[4]

Many people who know of my interest in dreams have enriched my life by sharing such dreams with me. Three such dreams follow, plus one of my husband's and one of my own.

Our Extraordinary Dreams

The first is one of a series of dreams Jose experienced over a long period many years ago. She calls them "life dreams." The first is entitled "A Rosy Amber Light." She lives in the Bay Area in California.

> I awaken, not knowing where I am, filled with a feeling of the most incredible sweetness. I say sweetness, yet the word is not enough to say what this feeling is—a feeling of incredible joy and beauty. This sensation sweeps through me— permeates me, and I don't know where I am. There is a glow everywhere—a rosy, golden light. Then I realize I am *inside* the body of a whale. Being inside the body was so sweet a feeling that the rosy, amber glow within the whale was like the glow of life. It was like being in a sculptured cavern of a citadel that glowed within. The main thing that was so incredible was the quality of the light, which was one with the ecstasy of sensation—it was a wonderful, glowing, comfortable, natural light of a rosy gold color, which seemed to both heal and unify the mind and the body. The measure of that sweetness and the rightness of that feeling continue in my life to be a refocusing point—something I can have through life to help and guide me.

This next one was shared with me by a student from Arkansas after a trip to the northwest by himself. I met him in Kentucky. Where he went after that I do not know. He was an intense and energetic person, searching for something. He calls his dream, "An Orb Swinging from the Starry Sky."

> In this dream I am in a mountainous place like the northwest part of the United States. There is fine green grass and fir trees standing in a semicircle. There is a feeling of being surrounded and protected by all creation. I'm in a Jeep and I stop. There is silence except for crickets chirping. I feel excitement and fear. It is all very mysterious—like being in touch with mystery. It is night. The stars stand out against the blackness. An elongated sphere, an orb, is swinging back and forth from the sky. A distinguished-looking watch chain connects the orb to a shadowy hand that comes from behind a black shadowy screen. There is a voice. The voice says "Look toward the light and not the darkness." It is a warm, awesome, gracious voice. I think of what it said as being directions for my life.

Part Six: Dreams Today

Then I see a tapestry-like thing. It is like a picture of anthropology. It is smooth as mud in light brown and earth tone colors, with plants, animals, dinosaurs, mammals, birds on it. I am afraid. The scene begins moving—moving faster and faster— until it shows a desert scene. Now I'm viewing early western history in past, present, and future.

The next is from a sermon by John Claypool, a minister friend whom I have known for a good many years. He shared this with his congregation in Jackson, Mississippi, January 22, 1978.

In this dream I was in an operating room. My spirit did come out of my head and was up on the ceiling, and I did see very vividly people with masks on and dressed in green gowns, working feverously over the body I recognized as my own. Then I moved out into a dark, cool corridor and felt that I was being carried by a current of air. I remember feeling no pain or apprehension, but rather a sense of excitement as to what was going to happen next.

Then I slid into what can best be described as "kindly light." It was warm and accepting, bright enough to be radiant, but not so bright as to hurt my eyes, and I recall being literally suffused by a sense of well-being and welcome. I saw no images, but I instinctively knew that this kindly light was God Himself. A voice from somewhere welcomed me and then said: "Let's go over your life and see what can be learned from it."

First He said: "Tell me, can you weep over all the pain you have caused other people, those things you have done that you wish you had not done or left undone that you ought to have done?" And with that, certain vivid memories out of my past began to come before my eyes, and I remember starting to cry, deep, soul-wrenching sobs, as the pain that I had brought into being began to materialize before me. I found this to be an anguish of the most acute sort. Someone once commented that the prodigal son in Jesus' parable got off too easily when he came home and all his father did was embrace him and give a party. "There should have been some kind of punishment, some form of retribution," this person agreed. However, another said in response to this, "I think the reality of punishment did take place. When that boy came limping home and the old father came running to meet him and got close enough to embrace him, the prodigal looked and saw the creases in that face and lines around the eyes, and suddenly realized what his sin had cost the grand old man who loved him so. You talk about punishment—this is worse than a thousand lashes." And as I wept in my dream, I understood more deeply the meaning of that insight. I wept as I have never wept before, and it seemed to me the kindly light about me wept also in tears almost too poignant to bear.

After a long period of this sort of thing, I remember a shift in mood, and the light said: "Let me ask you something else. Can you laugh? Do you remember all the good jokes you heard? Do you remember all the hilarious times you had? Do you remember the fool mistakes you have made that didn't hurt anybody else, but were signs of your bumbling?" And in response to that question, I remember seeing other moments in my life that had been amusing, and the laughter began—deep, belly laughs that came from a place as far down as the tears. And once again, it seemed as if the kindly light were laughing with me. Can you imagine what the laughter of God would sound like? There is no way I can put it into words, yet I have a feeling of it that touches me even now.

After a long period the laughter subsided and everything was quiet. And I remember the light said: "Let me ask you one more thing. Do you want anymore of it? Do you want to take what you have learned and go on living?" There was a time in my life that I would have regarded such a question as unnecessary. That was when I was young and assumed that everybody who was sick wanted to be well and that everybody who was alive wanted to remain so. However, since then I have felt the death wish often within myself. I have had moments when I was so sick of life, so fatigued, so disillusioned, and so frustrated that I wanted more than anything in the world to slip into the Nothingness forever and cease to be. So I did not answer at first; I really pondered the question, "To be or not to be?" Which of these did I really want? Then I remember saying: "You know, for all its pain and disappointment and imperfection, life is a gift, at bottom, worth all the struggle." And I remember saying with exuberance: "Yes, I really would like some more of it!" And with that, the light said: "All right, then," and I awoke.

The background for this dream-experience occurred a few days before when his son, going into surgery, suffered a cardiac arrest after the anesthetic was administered. He experienced a spacial separation from his body and was able to look down at the efforts being made to resuscitate him.

Part Six: Dreams Today

While many of these out-of-the ordinary dreams seem to be experiences to cherish for themselves, this one compels the dreamer to do something with it. John says he thought about his dream for ten months, trying to integrate what it had made real to him back into his conscious living before sharing it in this sermon. Three things grew out of it: first, a lessening of the fear of death, instead thinking of it as a time of transition rather than a time of extinction; second, a reinforcement of his conviction that God is for us and not against us, that judgment is more like a flower show where judges evaluate and discern rather than a police court where the judges condemn or sentence; third, the dream pinpointed for him the important qualities that make for high humanness—the abilities to weep, to laugh, to celebrate, to see the high comedy of it all, to desire to live and to grow, and to adventure into the unknown. He suggested to his congregation that they be open to the dream-dimension of their lives, stating his belief that God is as much at work at night as He is in the day and that something of immense importance can and often does happen when we stop actively grappling with reality and enter into that other state we call sleep.

Here is a great dream my husband shared with me just recently. Could it be that he dreamed it just for me, since I was in the midst of writing this section on extraordinary dreams? As dreams usually deal with the dreamer's life, I doubt it, but the timing couldn't be more perfect. My husband calls this a serial dream, although it was dreamed on two different nights. The second night's dream seems to be a continuation of the first night's about the machine for a special-needs child. It is unique in other ways, too. Besides being lucid with vivid colors, it includes a definite taste. I've never before been told a dream in which the sense of taste was a symbol, and Perpetua's dream ("Dreams of Early Christian Martyrs") is the only one I recall reading that mentions taste. I'm going to start with what he calls "Yesterday's Dream," which is the way he told it to me.

Our Extraordinary Dreams

Yesterday morning I awoke from a dream about a machine that blended tastes. I bought it at an antique show, but I didn't know what it was. It had two tubes in it. It turned like a pepper mill. It had two colors of granules in it, like salt and pepper, but when I began to turn it, it spun out a very interesting kind of candy. I tasted it and it had a very distinctive taste. It seems that just before this happened, a voice had said that there was a machine invented for a special-needs child to enable him to vote for the decision of some philanthropic organization.

In today's dream, there is a song put into a machine that registers in color the decision of a special-needs child. The trustees of this child send in the child's vote in yellow. When they put the color in the machine, I hear the song and see it with the background of yellow. It is a happy song, but I am puzzled at what this all means when one of the other trustees says, "Well, shall we play it in another color?" It starts to play in blue and then changes to deep plum. I realize that there could be other combinations of colors. Then one trustee said, "No, we don't have time for all that." I didn't actually see any trustees or a child. After I woke up, [He thinks he is awake, but he keeps on dreaming] I completed the dream with the thought of "This machine could be exploited and this child could be thwarted." Then as I get up I think to myself, "Yes, I'm trying to put it all together—come to some resolution. Yes, I want it all together. At my funeral I want some of my favorite pieces of art."

In my mind it it the same voice telling my about the candy machine of yesterday's dream. Now I remember that I had had a dream before this machine dream about Mack Price (owner of a shoe shop where Bill worked while going to college many years ago and where we had seen him in November last year). Mack is playing with children's toys and getting a big kick out of it. Then he faded away and was gone.

This dream came to my husband at a time when he was working intensely on a formal address to be presented to his colleagues. The address was on religion and the arts and related to integrating them. He had just completed it with the comment that it had all fallen together. This background explains some of the imagery, but much of the dream is a mystery.

In August 1980, one year after coming to the Bay Area, we moved into the foggiest area of San Francisco; it had been a foggier-than-usual summer and now it was a cold, drizzly winter. I had been depressed and unable to sleep. A doctor had

Part Six: Dreams Today

given me a prescription to promote sleeping. As I caught up on sleep, I caught up on dreaming. The following is one of my own extraordinary dreams. I call it "The Gray Sabbath Rabbit," and I dreamed it on New Year's night. My husband, a friend, and I had just seen the movie *Going in Style* starring George Burns.

I am looking at the front covers of a stack of magazines. The covers are colorful. They are painted in swirls. A woman's head has swirling hair. Scenic views have trees with swirling branches. As I come to magazines that are older, the covers have more and more gray in them until finally the covers are all gray. One magazine opens and takes us into a totally gray country (not black and white). I say "us" because now there is a small group of us, and we are children.

A kind old man wearing baggy comfortable clothes is our guide. He looks like George Burns. He isn't so gray as our environment. His trousers are lighter—almost white—and his coat or sweater is kind of a grayish purplish brown, mauve I guess. He has a walking stick that he uses as a pointer.

We walk slowly as a group. There is no sound from any of us nor from our environment in this strange new country. We see breathtaking scenes of soil, rock, and water formations. All this is dark gray and of the same texture, which is powdery looking, yet solid to the touch. There are areas that look like flowing water, but they do not flow. All the land formations can be recognized from their shapes, but they are this same powdery- looking solid substance. Plants look like the skeleton stalks and fragments one sees in the winter. They are dark and rigid, but are in positions that suggest movement.

We walk in a hushed manner up hills and down valleys, following winding paths until we come to a most unusual rock formation with a round hole in it. The guide speaks now and says, "The Sabbath rabbit is about to appear." This is all he says. We watch with quiet anticipation, and a gray rabbit's head slowly appears in the round opening. His head is framed by the almost round rock, which looks like a doughnut with an extra large hole. In fact I see now that it is very much like a frame. The gray rabbit looks at us and wiggles his nose slowly. Ordinarily this might have made me laugh, but these look like serious nose wiggles to me. We watch quietly as he slowly and regally hops around from behind the rock frame and stands full-bodied before us. We stand frozen with awe in his presence. This feels like a "once in an eternity" event. He disappears slowly and with dignity into the rock formations. We walk on with our guide.

Our Extraordinary Dreams

> I ponder the meaning of such an experience and why we were permitted to have it. I see that others in the group go on as if nothing has happened. I wonder how they can do this. And I wonder why our guide does not explain this or at least comment on it.

I awake and, realizing I've been dreaming, try to recall it without moving and sort of fall back asleep into dreaming. I dream, "Maybe we each have to discover our own meaning as with a dream."

At the time I understood little about this dream except that it depicted upheaval, depression, the passing of time. Gradually I understood the Sabbath Rabbit to be myself taking time out for adjusting to relocation and health difficulties, and the kind guide was giving me permission. I felt that in a way the kind guide was God showing me it was all right to be the way I was right then. Perhaps God looked like George Burns because George Burns played God in the movie, *Oh God*.

I'm often asked if God appears in dreams. Dream images such as a light, a voice, a hand from the heavens, even a figure who has characteristics that we attribute to God symbolize God in our dreams. I say the kind guide who looks like George Burns in my dream takes on the character of God. This is not to say that I see in George Burns characteristics that I attribute to God. I am just saying that the figure looked this way, probably since I had seen George Burns play God in the movie. The kind guide has some characteristics that I attribute to God: mystery, kindness, wisdom, healing. Even then I cannot say that he was God. I'm comfortable saying that the total impact of the dream experience was like an encounter with God.

God does not often take a form in a dream. Usually he remains unseen. When he appears in dreams, it does not have to be a visual appearance or even a vocal appearance. Most often he appears through the influence or the impact of the total dream experience, so that we feel like saying, "I was impressed through this dream that God wants me to consider doing thus and so." Only the dreamer can say what or who represents God in his/her dream.

Part Six: Dreams Today

A young teacher, who had once served in the Peace Corps in India, told me of a dream she had in which there was an image of a pupil and his father. The father was wearing light-colored, Indian-like clothing, but it was somehow different. In telling the dream, she used the term "father and son" and described them as religious. I wondered if this could be a symbol for God the Father and Jesus the Son. I did not ask outright, but conversation with her did not give me this impression. Instead she arrived at the conclusion that she had not given the spiritual side of her life much attention and she thought that perhaps this dream was suggesting that she give this some consideration. This was a case where my understanding and her understanding of the dream were different. Even had I been right she may not have been ready yet for that interpretation. Her understanding led her more gently into the direction of spiritual growth, allowing her to discover things for herself.

It is appropriate to discuss religious images here because when these images appear in dreams people often regard them as out of the ordinary. Not all of the images are from the Bible or from our religious practices. Some are non-religious but take on a religious meaning because of the way they are used in the dream, as in "My Heavenly Blue Kitten Dream" (page 156). On the other hand, some images from the Bible may take on a non-religious meaning with reference to waking life. I had a dream before moving from San Francisco to Louisville, Kentucky, in which I saw a white sheet in the sky over a body of water. It was filled with water and shorebirds, some of which were fluttering over and around it. Although modified it reminded me of Peter's vision (Acts 11:5-11). However, the dream did not deal with a change in belief systems as Peter's did. In the context of the dream, I understood it to be a symbol for "vision." It represented the vision I had of living in California, which I was giving up by moving. (The dream also included a collection of bluebirds fluttering close to a green, grassy terrain, which seemed to carry the promise of happiness in a new location.)

Our Extraordinary Dreams

When pastors, priests, and religious church leaders appear in dreams, they may represent a characteristic of the dreamer that is similar to a person of that occupation or to the specific person of that occupation. Or they may represent a part of yourself you need to develop or some practice needed in your life, such as confessing, forgiving, ministering. These are but a few suggestions. Only you can determine what the images mean in your dreams.

Religious objects and rituals appear in dreams, too; the ritual of baptism is one of them. I am surprised at how often some form of this practice appears in dreams. The following, entitled "Mexican Boy's Baptism," is my own.

> A little Mexican boy is going to some kind of a church activity like School. When he returns, he talks about being baptized each day. We don't know whether it's his inability to express himself in English or if he really is being baptized daily. We try to find out by asking him more about it. He was baptized once, so we think he is playing in water and calling it being baptized or maybe even playing like he is being baptized when he's playing in the water. Yet he insists that he is not playing. He says he has to be baptized everyday before he will be allowed to play and do other things. I decide to visit to see for myself what is going on. My husband keeps telling me what to wear, and I keep saying I don't like what he chooses. There's usually something a little strange about what he suggests. He tries to hang things on me—a scarf, a piece of jewelry, a hat—I say I'm tired of him trying to hang things on me.

More than a year before my dream, my husband had the following dream, entitled "Conflict of Interests."

> I am in a combat setting with British soldiers fighting Italian soldiers in Italy. The Italian young men and women are dressed in sports uniforms. So are the British, but they wear long pants instead of short ones. My assignment is to cut off the water supply and poison the water. There is not much time to do this. My vehicle bogs down in the mud and I can't get it out. A British chaplain, who reminds me of Clasper (Dean of St. John's Cathedral in Hong Kong), appears and wants to baptize some Italian religious people. This presents a problem as I want to help the chaplain. I manage to let

Part Six: Dreams Today

the chaplain baptize and also to cut off the water supply and poison it. I wake up feeling good that I've been able to carry out my assignment.

A young woman shared this one, which is about a deceased love one. It is called "A Rude Awakening."

> One week before the sixth month anniversary of Mother's death, I had a dream.
> I am at my parents home in Georgia and in their bedroom. I am snuggled up with blankets and pillows in their bed. I am looking at old family pictures. I look up at the wall and think, "Daddy is changing the pictures on the wall." I don't know if he is taking pictures down or putting new pictures up. It is like he is in process. I wonder if the pictures on the wall are a good idea.
> I hear mother call "Jane?" as she is coming from downstairs, as if she is wondering where I am and what I am doing. She sees me in their bedroom and comes in. She first throws a pillow at the foot of the bed as if she is going to lay down with me and look at the pictures with me. This is something I used to enjoy doing with her.
> Friskie, my mother's cat, is in the room, going crazy, playing and crawling up under the top layer of covers like cats will do.
> I look up to see mother standing across the room. She looks so beautiful. I know when I see her that she is Spirit, yet very real and present with me. Her hair is beautiful. She is dressed in an off-white to beige gown with sparkles in it like an evening gown. The gown is long-sleeved with no sewn seams. The gown covers her feet and sort of disappears into the floor, spirit-like.
> I look down to the picture the I am holding in my hand. It is a rather large black and white picture of mother's baptism at age seventeen. She is young and pretty. The picture is like some of the pictures of my mother I have seen of her when she was young, but I have never seen a picture of her baptism. She is dressed in a white dress. As I look at the picture, the picture takes action. I see mother very happy, walking down a crowded hill to a river to be baptized. Before she reaches the river, a man picks her up over his head and another man throws a bucket of water on her. She screams in surprise.

I wake up, puzzled about this rude awakening. The dream is too real and beautiful to end in such a crude way.

The strange thing to me about this dream is not so much the men's behavior at the end but that it reminds me of a baptism described to me by a person who had been baptized with water being thrown on her by the religious group she had belonged to in India. Jane did not know of this manner of baptism nor did she think her mother did. She, as with my husband and myself, had been baptized by immersion, being lowered into the water and brought up again to symbolize being buried to the old way of life and risen to a new way of life. (This is also a way of making public confession of one's acceptance of Jesus as Christ and son of God as well as an act of commitment; a more universal meaning would be "cleansing" and "a new beginning.")

Baptisms by immersion were done in rivers before plumbing and the use of indoor baptisteries. "River" seems to have additional meaning because of its association with physical death in literature. We often use "crossing over the river" in poetry to symbolize death and entrance into a new life. An example of this is in the following American folk hymn:

> On Jordan's stormy banks I stand
> And cast a wishful eye,
> To Canaan's fair and happy land
> Where my possessions lie.
>
> All o'er those wide extended plains
> Shines one eternal day;
> There God the Son forever reigns
> And scatters night away.
>
> No chilling winds nor pois'nous breath
> Can reach that healthful shore;
> Sickness and sorrow, pain and death
> Are felt and feared no more.

The end of Jane's dream may have referred to Jane rather than to her mother. The dash of water symbolized "a rude awakening" to the reality of her mother's death and her own beginning of a life without her.

I have just recently become aware of baptism as a symbol in dreams and plan to further explore its use in dreams.[5]

Part Six: Dreams Today

One Presbyterian minister has worked with dreams in his congregation, observing personal dream imagery and events in connection with the biblical materials. They found that we can learn much about the nature of dreaming, dream language, and the origin and function of symbols from such a study. The following are some of their observations about symbolic imagery:

1. Attending to dreams frequently links us directly with biblical imagery when symbols from the text appear in like form in our dreams.

2. Dream interpretation, by making us consciously aware of our inner imagery, helps distinguish our private images of God from the biblical images.

3. Dream interpretation trains us to take specific imagery of biblical language seriously and ask why a particular symbol is used instead of another, which we should do with dream-symbols that confront us in our own dreams.

4. Attending to dreams moves people from "reading the Bible" to participation in its living symbols.

5. Symbols heal the soul and make it able to "tolerate history" by overcoming lack of meaning.

6. The very similarity of the two worlds of symbolism, which hold promise of a vital link between them, hold also the danger of confusion between them.

7. Dream interpretation can lead to exclusive preoccupation with "inner meanings" of the biblical language and a corresponding loss of interest in its sociological implications.

8. Dream interpretation may ignore the historical circumstances of the dream. This is a barrier to understanding all dreams, both biblical and personal.[6]

Other dreams experienced as unusual by the dreamer, but really not so uncommon, are *dreams in which a deceased loved one appears* not long after the loved one's death. These are sometimes dreams that develop into waking visions. These dreams are often part of the grieving process and are comforting. "... such experiences are healing acts of God."[7]

Dreams in which the deceased loved one appears have been frequently reported in literature. An author gathered such selections from literature into a book to help her in her grief over her husband's sudden death. She wrote of her experience in poetry. This is the introduction to the poem.

> The night of my husband's death as I packed clothes to take to the funeral home, impulsively I placed in a pocket a snapshot of our last island vacation together, a time of particular happiness. This image was returned to me several months later in a dream.[8]

She also writes that some of these dreams leave the dreamer feeling bereft, "as if our unconscious is reminding us that we have not yet fully accepted the cruelty of the loss or have feelings still to be resolved." She includes excerpts from Edmund Wilson's private journal, which records eight such dreams over a period of about four years after his wife's death in an accidental fall.[9] Clearly they reflect unresolved feelings and inability to accept her death.

The dreams I've been privileged to have shared with me usually picture the loved one as well and healthy, in no pain or discomfort, and are frequently humorous. There is also an element of comfort in knowing of the continued existence of the departed one. Sometimes the dreamer is actually comforted by words and gestures of the deceased. I've related one such dream of my own in the preface of this book. Four other more recent accounts follow.

Part Six: Dreams Today

When Josie's father died about a year ago, she experienced two dreams in which he appeared. Both dreams were pleasant and he looked well. He commented on having just been through an incredible experience and said he couldn't stay long because he was "steaming." As he talked of "steaming," his body vanished until only his head was left and then it, too, vanished. We both laughed gently and agreed that "steaming" meant becoming vapor, and therefore spirit, and described his new dimension of existence.

A woman whom I met recently, only six weeks after her husband's death, told me of her daughter's dream. Her father appeared in her dream well and happy, although he had been through a long illness. He told her he couldn't stay long and had to see the mortician to have his nose fixed. "The mortician has done a lousy job with my nose," he said. This man had a large nose, characteristic of the American Indian side of his family, and was described as having a sense of humor. His wife said this was just the sort of thing he might say.

A student tells of a dream-like experience two months following the death of his parents, who had been murdered. He was asleep at first and woke up feeling as though his whole body was in a painful spasm like a "charley horse." He heard a swishing sound like wind blowing and his father's voice saying, "Everything is all right. Not to worry." In the background he could hear his mother crying softly. Even though his mother was crying, he felt reassured and comforted.

Inventor and engineer Nathaniel Wyeth, on the TV program "A Smithsoniam World," tells of a dream he had right after his father's death. Nathaniel's father, N. C. Wyeth, was America's foremost illustrator by the time he was twenty-eight years old. He died in a tragic car accident. Nathaniel says, "I had a dream that I met father again. I shook his hand and said to him 'You don't know how great a person you were.' I kept shaking his hand. When I woke up I was shaking the bed covers."

Our Extraordinary Dreams

One of N. C. Wyeth's artist daughters painted flowers the day after his death. They were the most beautiful flowers she had ever painted. She says she felt him instructing her from over her shoulder.

Such experiences are a mystery.

Predictive dreams provoke not only wonder but fear. My friend, Jeanette, shared one with me in a letter. It provoked more wonder than fear.

> I had a vivid dream that came true. I dreamed our car was caved in on the left side—and now it is in exactly the same place. Mrs. S. backed into it on the parking lot. So what kind of dream foretells?

Such dreams are difficult to understand for at least two reasons. First, some dreams seem to be predictive but aren't; and second, there are at least two kinds of predictive dreams.

The first kind of dream gives data about the future that can be tested against the reality of later events. Pharaoh had such a dream. To Pharaoh it gave information about the famine to come and was of practical value in saving human life, warning him to store up grain for the leaner years. Later events gave proof of this. The second kind of dream speaks of God's ultimate and eternal purpose. Sometimes they are both woven into the same dream as in Pharaoh's dream.

Quite often predictive dreams are difficult to understand in that it isn't clear why the dreamer has them. This is especially so when they convey a warning. The dreamer feels there's nothing that can be done about the information, that even if she/he tries to intervene, she/he would not be taken seriously and would not be able to stop the people involved from going on with their plans. Nor do I personally know of circumstances being altered that were revealed in a dream so that the event dreaded would not come to pass, although we do see it done in biblical dreams. Perhaps if all the parties involved valued dreams, events could be altered. Biblical dreamers, whether they were believers in the One Living God or pagan gods, all seemed to value dreams, dreams of others as well as their own. The following is a predictive- type dream, but it is doubtful that

Part Six: Dreams Today

the dreamer could have done anything to prevent the catastrophe. For reasons we don't understand, a person who is not involved directly sometimes dreams about a terrible event before it happens. It may be a means of calling attention to the importance of dreams. This is just as Beth has written.

> It was close to 2:30 a.m., Monday, January 27, 1986, when I awoke from the nightmare. It was not until the space shuttle exploded that I associated the dream with that tragedy. I had been watching and listening to news broadcasts of the preparations that week with special interest because the teacher, Christa McAuliffe, was part of the astronautical team.
>
> The dream was very strange, and as I remember it, it was almost completely silent until the very end. I was teaching in one of the seminar rooms at school, which is a room with several large tables so that students can work together in small groups rather than the traditional classroom setting. I was teaching with Marjorie Stelmach, a friend and fellow English teacher, which seemed natural at the time, but we have never taught together. Suddenly we were called to the basement—there was no announcement that I can remember, we just knew to proceed as if it were some kind of emergency drill.
>
> Then we were in the basement and Dr. Bob Bannister, an assistant principal, wanted my class to go back upstairs. He was wearing a party hat, like the ones worn at a child's birthday party, except a little larger. As we processed out the door, he placed a party hat on each of us. Marjorie did not come with us.
>
> We were again in the classroom, but now the walls were glass and it was nighttime. The room moved up, like a giant elevator. It stopped, doors opened and Marjorie walked in. The room started to ascend again, and this time stars were everywhere, I turned to Marjorie, who had a terrified look on her face, and said, "What is it?" She replied, "We are about to witness..." and I cannot remember her exact words. She said something like a terrible explosion.
>
> The impact her words had on me was so great that I couldn't really remember—it was then that I awakened with my heart racing. I was sweating—almost in a panic and terribly distressed. I have had a few ESP experiences before, and I felt strongly that this dream was supposed to mean something. I thought it meant nuclear war.

Our Extraordinary Dreams

I called my husband, who was on call at the hospital. I was really scared, and it shook him up a little bit, too. We even talked about what we would do if a nuclear explosion occurred. He tried to calm me, but I couldn't go back to sleep. I felt such a sense of urgency, but I couldn't explain it or understand it.

At school that morning, I ran into Marjorie on the way to my room. She immediately noticed that something was wrong, which surprised me. I told her about the dream, even though I was afraid that she would think I was crazy. She told me that she, too, had a dream about nuclear war, which certainly did not make me feel any better. I felt like I had had twenty cups of coffee and was nervous and distracted all day. I told two of my students about the dream also.

While driving to work Tuesday morning, I heard on the news that the shuttle flight had again been postponed for a few minutes.

I felt less distressed by this time, but the dream had made quite an impact on me. I had not forgotten it.

Later that morning, as I walked out of the very classroom that had been in in my dream, one of the students that I had talked to about the dream ran up to me and said, "Mrs. Swann, did you hear the news?" "What news?" "The space shuttle...it blew up!"

I couldn't believe it. I was shocked. Then as the students said, "Remember your dream? Maybe that was it—the explosion." I felt sick, and at the same time I felt relief. Of course I was horrified, but because it had not been nuclear war, I was relieved. Next, I felt guilty...guilty for feeling relief at the announcement of the tragedy and also for feeling as if I knew about it and couldn't prevent it.

I tried to discount it as coincidence, but I had already convinced myself. My feelings were too strong, and there were other little "coincidences" that made sense with the dream. Dr. Bannister was the one who made the announcement Tuesday afternoon when it was official that it was doubtful that any of the astronauts had survived. He called for a moment of silence. That was the only announcement he made all year—he's the only administrator who never makes announcements. Also, it wasn't until Wednesday that I learned from my husband that the children in Christa McAuliffe's class had been wearing party hats at the time they watched the liftoff and explosion.

It was a long time before I could bring myself to watch the taped version of the explosion on TV—and I felt sick when I finally did. I still feel strange whenever I think about it.

Part Six: Dreams Today

Telepathic dreams, dreams of events that take place at the moment of dreaming, are also difficult to understand. There are two kinds: personal and impersonal. I have not had either kind; however, people have told me of dreaming of the death of a relative to learn later that the dream occurred at the time of the death. This is the personal kind. I have read of those who have dreamed of some terrible accident involving those they didn't know at the time of the accident. Descriptions of the disaster or a photograph in the newspaper would coincide with the setting of the dream. This impersonal type of dream is like the seemingly predictive dream of the space shuttle tragedy. The personal kind may be a way of preparing us for something totally unexpected. Still others may be for different reasons.

Lou, who is a great dreamer and had already had one dream in which her husband had an aura around his head, had an amusing telepathic dream. Her husband was in a city some distance away attending a conference. In her dream she saw a woman taking up a lot of her husband's time. She could see what she looked like and how she dressed. The woman was wearing a lot of green stuff, either a scarf or jewelry, around her neck. When her husband returned home the next night, she asked him if any woman had been taking too much of his time at the conference. He replied in surprise that he had been annoyed by a woman who was wearing a lot of turquoise jewelry and who had been using too much of his conference time and that he had to discourage her.

Dreams with elements of telepathy, clairvoyance, and prediction often produce anxiety, and there is a question about how we should treat such dreams. Although there are exceptions that the dreamer sometimes recognizes at the time of dreaming, a good general rule to follow is "...when we receive what seems like an unusual dream, we first relate to it as if it were an ordinary dream, that is, we do dreamwork on it as we would any other dream, but remain open to the possibility the dream may be more than an ordinary dream, that is it may also be speaking to another level of reality."[10]

Conclusion

> Everything that God has created is good; nothing is to be rejected, but everything is to be received with a prayer of thanks (1 Timothy 4:4 TEV).

I hope that sharing the exploration of my religious dream heritage will be valuable to the reader in the study of biblical, early church, and personal dreams.

Dream traditions of the early Christian church and ordinary, everynight dreams complete the exploration into my ancient Jewish and early Christian dream heritage. However, dreaming did not stop there. People in both Jewish and Christian traditions always valued dreams for their personal use and for their community's use. Unfortunately, dreams soon fell into disuse after Jerome's time. This was for a variety of reasons that are outside the scope of this book.[1]

It was not until the early twentieth century, when Sigmund Freud published his psychiatric research in a book entitled *The Interpretation of Dreams*, that the importance of dreams was brought to our attention again. Even then, they were not considered a means of communication between the spiritual and physical worlds, nor an encounter with God, nor a means of spiritual growth. We are indebted to Freud, for bringing dreaming to our attention again, and to Carl Jung, for relating dreams to the spiritual and religious aspects of life. From Jung we have learned much about methods and principles of working

Conclusion

with dreams. The methods are compatible with biblical as well as psychological traditions. Still, Jung's theories, along with Freud's, must be considered part of the psychological tradition rather than the religious because they mainly focus on personality, health, and development.

Morton Kelsey and John Sanford are most responsible for returning dreams to their valuable state in regard to Christians and their community. Kelsey and Sanford also refocused our attention on the place of dreams in the Bible and early church history. Both men are clergymen and counselors. They are leading researchers of the place of dreams in the Bible and the use of dreams in the area of spiritual counseling. They have shared their knowledge and skills generously through writing and speaking. I am especially grateful to Morton Kelsey for his books, his lectures, and his personal encouragement.

It is only now that biblical scholars are beginning to study biblical and early church dream traditions and to deal with contemporary dreams directly from them. I've referred to several of their works in this book. I especially appreciate the work of Louis Savary, which develops dreamwork techniques based on biblical and early church practices, combined with psychological insights and contemporary research.

We are created in such a way that visions come to us while we sleep (and sometimes when we are awake). This is something all people in all places and ages have in common. Everyone dreams unless prevented by some means, such as by researchers in sleep laboratories or by certain drugs. And these are only temporary conditions. However, some individuals do "lack the normal capacity to discharge emotional tensions through words, gestures, or symbols (including dreams)."[2]

In 1953, scientists proved that everyone dreams nightly. Until that time, some people who did not recall their dreams did not believe that they dreamed. Scientists also discovered rapid eye movement, or REM, which is associated with dreaming.

Conclusion

So now we know that the biological activity of dreaming is a scientific fact, but what about the content of these visions we have while asleep? How should we value these? As amusing breakfast conversation? As unreal or meaningless? As waste products of brain activity that should be disregarded? Perhaps the big problem in our Western culture is our definition of *real*. We tend to think in terms of only one kind of reality, or if we think in terms of more than one reality, we value one above the other.[3] Usually we consider real only what we can see, touch, or experience with our senses. Even those who affirm a spiritual/non-physical/non-material reality do not affirm or know how to handle dreams as part of that reality. Comments such as "It must have been the pizza I ate last night"; "I know it's just a dream"; and "I never dared tell anyone this dream before" are examples of the difficulty people have in accepting dreams as one way of being in touch with non-physical reality.

Laurens van der Post in *Jung and the Story of Our Time* (New York: Random House, Inc., 1975) tells of growing up in a home where the Bible was read and prayers were said daily, but was made to feel incompetent and isolated because of his dreams. After he was grown and had left the British army after World War II, he again felt isolated upon entering a "bitter, competitive world." He wondered what had happened to the great dreaming process he had discovered as a child, and he knew that somehow the world had to start dreaming again. But even his most perceptive contemporaries just laughed when he dared to mention such a thing to them.

In our continuing effort to understand physical and non-physical realities, we sometimes use the words *inner* and *outer* to distinguish between different realities. Again, we tend to value the outer reality over the inner reality. So where does such a system place dreams? Obviously in the less-preferred reality or in the altogether unreal.

Our regard for what is real and not real determines the value we place on dreams and their function and the way we understand and use them. If we consider the material world as the only reality, dreams are little appreciated. Even when we

Conclusion

believe in various dimensions of reality, some people are more rational in their thinking, and they thus find it difficult to value dreams in the same way as people who are more intuitive by nature. But even just a little attention to dreams and inner experiences can help bring about a balance in our lives.

In searching for balance in their lives, the biblical dreamers, with the exception of the non-Hebrew dreamers, were able to create a system of unity between dream life and waking life. They did this by considering dreams in the context of outer events. Dreams were real and important, but events surrounding them were just as important. Each contributed to the understanding of the other. We see this connection of dream reality and waking reality in Jacob's dream. The ladder with the angels ascending and descending between earth and heaven depicts matter and spirit as being connected—and parts of a greater reality. This view of dreams may partially explain why the Hebrew dreamers did not require interpretation of their experience. Both Pharaoh and Nebuchadnezzar valued their dreams, but perhaps they looked at their dreams to the exclusion of other conditions in their lives.

There is another way we might look at the place of dreams and visions in the Bible. Consider the amount of space devoted to dreams: If you start with the actual citations of dreams and visions, then add references made to them in events, discussions, and prophetic speaking, you will discover about a third of the content of the Bible consists of dreams, visions, and related material. Abraham Lincoln made a study of the place of dreams in the Bible after a dream he had before his assassination, in which he saw his own body lying in state in the White House. He observed, "How much there is in the Bible about dreams. There are, I think, some sixteen chapters in the Old Testament and four or five in the New in which dreams are mentioned; and there are many other passages scattered throughout the book which refer to visions."[4]

Conclusion

While this is not a book of methods and techniques for understanding dreams, I do suggest some ways of relating to dreams. Three ideas can be taken from the practices of the biblical dreamers and be used by us today.

First, conversation or dialogue with God suggests prayer as a means of understanding. Conversation with dream characters, such as the ancient dreamers had with the angels, is another good technique and is used by psychologists and those who work professionally with dreams today. Don't be afraid to ask even the unpleasant characters what they are doing in your dreams. Such conversation in your head can lead to some interesting insights.

Second, physically respond to the dream. Writing it and giving it a title honors the dream and may provide some understanding. Sketch a picture to illustrate it, or dramatize the different parts, objects as well as persons, or an idea the dream suggests. Once I dreamed of a pink stuffed cat, and that very week I saw one just like it in a craft shop. I purchased it, and eight years later it still brings me much pleasure as I recall the little English village where I found not only the cat, but a bit of understanding about myself as well. (I do not suggest that you buy all the things you dream about, though.) By physically responding to your dreams, you may discover ways to further react to them, such as making choices, approaching from a different perspective, or observing feelings in your waking life. Something as simple as taking a walk to celebrate the dream may be satisfying. This should not get to be a burden or something you think you have to do with every dream, or it may discourage dream recall as well as dreamwork. Both of these responses, writing and taking action, were practiced by the biblical dreamers.

Third, tell your dream to someone. Dream sharing with another individual or a group is one of the best ways to understand your dream. There are professionals trained to help others understand their dreams, but anyone who is open to the value of dreams can help. An outside person can notice elements in the dream as well as the way the dreamer tells the

Conclusion

dream that the dreamer, being so close to it, does not. My dream "Looking into the Pool" in chapter 24 is a good example of this. The listeners noticed how many times I used "look" and "see" to tell the dream. Calling this to my attention helped me understand the dream better.

The following is another example of how a group discussion helped me understand my dream, which I call "Space-Age Surgery."

> I am looking down from an observation place onto an operating room scene in a hospital. I see Dr. Sol and a small group of medical students standing around the operating table on which a patient lies. I don't really see the patient because of the students hovering around him or her and the table. The operating room is not cluttered with big machines and cords. There is only a small box hanging from a metal arm that can be swung around to change the position of the box. The box is no larger than a pocket-size instamatic camera, and it has a cone attached to one end. The cone is attached at the point to the box. I am observing a remarkable surgical procedure. No injections, anesthesia, and no cutting are used. The surgery is done by rays that are invisible and controlled by this streamlined box-like device. In fact, it is surgery and healing all together with no need for recovery time.

I shared this with my dreamwork group led by Dr. Gayle Delaney. The following questions helped me understand the dream.

Do you have any idea what this dream means?
I have no idea.

Describe the setting again.
It is a hospital operating room—lighted, but not bright—with none of the cumbersome equipment or tangle of cords. The doctor wore a white office coat. The students wore regular street clothing. None wore the usual green surgical garb.

Conclusion

Does this remind you of anything in your life?
I've had laser surgery on my tongue, and Dr. Sol Silverman cared for me afterward and took pictures for use in his teaching.

Who is Dr. Sol?
Dr. Sol is Dr. Sol Silverman, who did post-operative care. He teaches oral surgery. He works gently, explaining quietly what he is doing. He's warm and considerate and yet you know that he is very skilled. We have a trusting doctor-patient relationship.

What is special about this medical box operated by Dr. Sol in the dream?
It utilizes the healing elements from the atmosphere. It picks them up and channels them to the needed spot.

What in this dream is like something in your waking life?
The laser used for my tongue surgery and Dr. Sol and his camera. (Here I had a block about seeing beyond the factual or seeing the factual as a metaphor for something in my life.)

What kind of operation is it that restores function or promotes healing or well-being but requires no anesthesia, injections, or cutting and no recovery period?
(Something begins to click in my thinking.) Could it be dreamwork? That's it! The box represents dreams. The medical students are those in my dream-sharing group. Dr. Sol is really Gayle, who directs the operations of the group. Also, "Sol" stands for sun, from which healing waves come. Dr. Sol Silverman, Dr. Gayle Delaney, the sun, and dreams all radiate warmth and are channels of healing.

Along with these three ideas, I strongly urge the practice of thinking of the dream in the context of the outer events in your life. Think of the dream as one of your experiences—not any

Conclusion

more or less important than the others. All of our experiences, inner and outer, are connected and enrich the understanding of the other.

Finally, I suggest the use of the principles by Robert Johnson in his book *Inner Work*, which I have abbreviated below:

FOUR PRINCIPLES OF VALID INTERPRETATION

1. *Choose an interpretation that shows you something you didn't know—that challenges your existing ideas.*

"Remember, the main function of a dream is to communicate something to you that you don't know, that you are unaware of...to challenge you, help you grow, wake you up to what you need to learn and where you need to change."

Exception: When dreams *seem* to be sending the same basic message over and over again, ask why the dream has to keep repeating the message—either you don't understand or won't put it into practice.

2. *Avoid the interpretation that inflates your ego.*

"Dreams function as reporters." They will report back to you when you have made change or advanced in development. When they do, "you have a right to feel pleased"; however, if you find yourself congratulating yourself on how wonderful you are, how high above other mortals, then your interpretation is not accurate.

3. *Avoid interpretation that shifts responsibility away from yourself.*

Your dreams are not concerned with pointing out the faults of other people, or where other people need to change. Your dreams are concerned with *you*: If your dream comments on an external situation, it will focus on the contributions of *your* attitudes and unconscious behavior patterns.

Conclusion

4. *Learn to live with dreams over time—fit them into the long- term flow of your life.*

The full meaning of some dreams only becomes clear with the passage of time. "If, after all your work, you can't honestly choose one definitive interpretation of your dream, then consent to live with it for a while." Be able to say (after you worked with the dream), "it may mean this, or it may mean that. It may go this way, or it may go another way, only time will tell....Give yourself time and experience, keep interacting with the symbols, return to the dream from time to time...."[5]

Ordinary, everynight dreams are important, too—even those we don't remember. Unrecalled dreams renew us psychologically and promote our emotional well-being in ways that we don't understand yet. When a dream is recalled it becomes significant. Dreams signal us to pay attention to something, usually ourselves. When we do pay attention to them, the dreams can promote growth and guide us in our day to day living.

Dreams can have religious meaning as well as personal meaning. Paying attention to them gives us an additional resource in both areas. While thy may not be as dramatic as some of the Biblical dreams or other extraordinary dreams, neither are they dull. It is worthwhile to work with our ordinary dreams for their value to us. The more we've learned to appreciate these, the better prepared we are when confronted with an extraordinary dream in which we meet God.

Notes

INTRODUCTION

Ancient Near Eastern Dream Practices

1. A. Leo Oppenheim, "Interpretation of Dreams in the Ancient Near East," *Transactions of the American Philosophical Society* (Philadelphia: American Philosophical Society, 1956), 186-187, 206-207, 209-210.

I am indebted to Mr. Oppenheim for much of this background material. Unless otherwise identified, all quotations are from this source.

This and the notes that follow are from research done after my personal study of dreams in the Bible; however, having discovered the additional background information, I felt that it enriched and confirmed my understanding and is of value to the reader who wishes to pursue a more in-depth study. I also appreciate knowing that others are studying various facets of the place dreams hold in the Bible.

2. Sleeping in sacred places to seek a dream was called incubation. Such dreams were rarely recorded until later Near Eastern times. Sometimes dreams were unintentionally incubated just by sleeping in a holy place, as occured with the boy Samuel (1 Samuel 3:1f.) and with Jacob (Genesis 28:10-11). An example of intentionally provoking the incubation of a dream is Solomon in Gibeon (1 Kings 3:5, also Chronicles 1:5). There is an interest in incubation today for both secular and religious purposes. For information on this, see the following books:

Gayle M. V. Delaney, *Living Your Dreams* (San Francisco: Harper & Row, Publishers Inc., revised 1988).

Notes

Louis M. Savary, Patricia H. Berne, and Strephon Kaplan Williams, *Dreams and Spiritual Growth* (New York/Ramsey: Paulist Press, 1984).

The contemporary dream incubation ritual does not require withdrawing to a temple as in ancient days. Some people practice it in the privacy of their own homes. Others may wish to separate themselves from the demands and cares of everyday living with a small group whose aim is to enter into a more special place or space. One example of this is the Wilderness Dream Quest backpacking retreat, conducted by a clinical psychologist. The participants use "dream incubation and sharing in a supportive group process to focus on important personal growth issues" and find them a "highly effective addition to the treatment program of psychiatric patients and delinquent and disadvantaged adolescents." It is also "a natural antidote to the stresses and routine of urban living" (Alan B. Siegel, "Dream Quest: A Wilderness Retreat," *Newsletter: Association for the Study of Dreams* 2[September 1985]:3).

3. Our Western culture has the idea that, in some nonliterate and primitive societies, culture pattern dreams (akin to biblical dreams or official dreams that affect the dreamer's culture) and personal dreams (ordinary dreams) are distinctly different. Waud H. Kracke is an associate professor of anthropology at the University of Illinois and has training in psychoanalysis. He believes this idea is a misconception on our part because we place greater emphasis on personal dreams while the more primitive societies emphasize their culture pattern dreams. They report their dream encounters, which include experiences with a supernatural being, in a way typical of their culture. This may lead us to believe they do not even have personal dreams. But Kracke maintains that such dreams do express personal desires and fears; it just takes someone skilled in asking tactful and sensitive questions to derive the personal meaning. He bases his belief on work he is doing with the indigenous Amazonian culture. (From an address to the Association for the Study of Dreams Conferences in 1986 on the "Cultural and Personal Meaning of Dreams.")

4. Dennis Pierce McEntire, "The Dream Report as a Literary Unit," Th.M. Thesis, Southern Baptist Theological Seminary, 1970.

McEntire compares the three-part pattern of Oppenheim's with a five-part pattern by Wolgang Richter (presented in an article in a German publication in the German language) and arrives at a four-part pattern. Oppenheim and Richter are the only two persons to detect specific patterns for dream reports. Richter discusses only dream reports of the Hebrew Bible, while Oppenheim discusses reports outside the biblical area.

Oppenheim sees the report of the simple message dream constructed with a frame and its content. The frame includes the introduction and conclusion and explains, among other circumstances, who, when, and where. Richter sees five parts in the dream report: introduction, opening formula, dream body, interpretation, and fulfillment.

McEntire outlines the symbolic dream message with the following parts:
1. *frame elements*: located before and after the dream body;
2. *opening formula*: a statement containing the word "behold," spoken by the dreamer, or "in my dream," and is followed by the dream itself;
3. *dream body*: contains images;
4. *interpretation*: examines and utilizes the images. This not only explains the meaning of the dream but neutralizes or dissolves the evil content intended for the dreamer when the dream is considered bad.

5. John Navone, S.J., "Dreams in the Bible," *The Bible Today*, November 1975.

PART ONE: DREAMS AND VISIONS IN THE HEBREW BIBLE

Chapter 2
Jacob: Dreams Preserve the Covenant People

1. Henry Reed, *Getting Help from Your Dreams* (Virginia Beach: Inner Vision Publishing Co., 1985) 5-14.

Chapter 4
Joseph and Daniel: Two Interpreters of Others' Dreams

2. Oppenheim, "Interpretations," 210.

3. *Great People of the Bible and How They Lived* (Pleasantville, NY: The Reader's Digest Association, Inc., 1974). Much of the background material in this section comes from this source. The reference to Joseph's coat is found on page 58.

4. Savary, et. al., *Dream and Spiritual Growth*, 120.

5. McEntire, "The Dream Report, 35.

Nebuchadnezzar tests the ability of the wise men to interpret dreams by their ability to recount the dream itself. The wise men's inability to do so and admitting that no one except the gods could do such a thing was in keeping

Notes

with common belief concerning the origin of symbolic dreams. This belief held that such a dream was from a deity and could, therefore, only be revealed by a deity.

6. Diane Keck, "Dreams and Vision," Research Associates at the New Wineskins Center in Columbus, Ohio.

7. Buckner B. Trawich, *The Bible as Literature* (New York: Barnes & Noble Books, 1973).

Chapter 5
A Criminal's Vision and Conversation with God

8. *Great People of the Bible*, 70.

The descendants of Joseph and his kinsman who settled in Goshen, Egypt, to escape the famine, lived peacefully and prosperously there for nearly four centuries. Then a new line of pharaohs (rulers) came into power and the Hebrews were made into slaves.

9. William Self and Carolyn Shealy, *Confessions of a Nomad* (Atlanta: Peachtree Publishers Ltd. 1983), 17, 21.

Chapter 7
A Midianite Soldier's Dream
Predicts Victory for Israel

10. Oppenheim, "Interpretations," 210.

Chapter 9
A Prophet Dreams a Message for the King

11. Robert Karl Gnuse, *The Dream Theophany of Samuel* (Lanham, MD: University of American, Inc. 1984), 86.

"'Dreamer of dreams' who seeks to lead Israel away from the Lord. It is difficult to determine if this deliberate apostasy was hyperbole on the author's part, or if the dreamers did advocate worship of other deities, such as a dream deity. So we cannot be certain if the passage condemned all dream diviners, including prophets of Israel who received dreams, or just a certain professional class, who might be more open to foreign influence and thus more liable to lead Israel to apostasy." Prophets thought they needed a confirming sign in order to speak—even false prophets can claim dreams as a confirming sign. "Thus the passage has a negative attitude toward dreams because of their association with false prophesy, be they either from foreign prophets or perverted prophets to Israel. Dreams were not rejected as a possible means of revelation, but one must be critical of them."

12. Welton Gaddy, "How to Identify a False Prophet," an unpublished sermon (Broadway Baptist Church, Fort Worth, Texas, February 21, 1982).

Chapter 10
A Dream as a Source of Wisdom

13. Oppenheim, "Interpretations," 188.

14. Ibid., 191.

Chapter 11
A Vision of God's Holiness

15. *Great People of the Bible*, 224f.

16. Notes from *The New English Bible with Apocrypha,* Oxford Study Edition (New York: Oxford University Press, 1976).

17. Trawich, *Bible As Literature,* 178.

Summary of
Dreams and Visions in the Hebrew Bible

18. Gnuse, *Dream Theophany,* 13.

19. Ibid., 21.

20. Albert L. Meiburg, "An Understanding of the Dream as a Means of Divine Revelation," Ph.D. diss. (Louisville, KY: Southern Baptist Theological Seminary, 1954), 22f.

21. Ibid., 29-31.

Notes

PART TWO: DREAMS AND VISIONS IN THE APOCRYPHA

Chapter 12
Dreaming in the Intertestamental Period

1. The Jews divided their sacred books into three groups: the Law, the Prophets, and the Writings. The books of the Law were the first to reach final form by about 300 B.C. The Prophets were concluded about 200 B.C., and the Writings were not finalized until A.D. 100. A number of books were left over. These were withdrawn from public use; therefore, they became known as the Apocrypha, which comes from a Greek word meaning "hidden." Only a select few read them.

2. See notes in the *New English Bible with the Apocrypha* for a more in-depth discussion of the Apocrypha.

3. Morton Kelsey, *God, Dreams, and Revelation* (Minneapolis: Augsburg Publishing House, 1974). Discussion of the Apocrypha, 74-42.

4. Trawich, *The Bible as Literature*, 360-361.

Chapter 13
A Persian Queen's Cousin Dreams and Saves the Jewish People

5. Reed, *Getting Help from Your Dreams*, 14.

PART THREE: DREAMS AND VISIONS IN THE NEW TESTAMENT

Chapter 14
Historical Background of New Testament Dreams

1. Kelsey, *God, Dreams, and Revelation*. I am indebted to Kelsey for this background material and suggest this book be read for a more complete discussion of the subject.

Notes

2. *Great People of the Bible*, 311.

Chapter 15
A Foster Father-to-be Dreams

3. Savary, et. al., *Dreams and Spiritual Growth*, 29.

4. Navone, "Dreams in the Bible."

"An angel is a messenger acting as God's agent actually seen as a visionary experience (who does not eat and drink) and sometimes appears as a concrete physical being who eats and converses" (Gen. 19:1f.).

5. Ibid.

Chapter 16
Jesus and Dreams

6. Wendy Doniger O'Flaherty, *Dreams, Illusions and Other Realities* (Chicago: The University of Chicago Press, 1984), 3.

7. Morton Kelsey, *Dreams: A Way to Listen to God* (New York: Paulist Press, 1978), 67.

8. M. Scott Peck, *People of the Lie,* (New York: Simon and Schuster Inc., 1983), 182-211.

"Demons and evil spirits" are those realities who try to take over and possess a human person and are able to do so.

Chapter 17
The Apostles and Dreams

9. Jeremy Taylor, *Dream Work,* (New York: Paulist Press, 1983), 123.

The special set of circumstances in Peter's dream has the element and quality of "synchronicity." Taylor's book is just one of many that discuss this. He defines synchronicity as seemingly random events resonant with and relating to each other and to a dream. He describes them as unnerving, eerie, inexplicable, spooky. He's persuaded that the primary function of such an "eerie connection" of waking life events to a dream is to call to mind the dream and to emphasize that the event is "particularly appropriate and symbolically resonant with some important drama in the dreamer's own life."

10. Kelsey, *God, Dreams, and Revelation*, 96-7.

Notes

Kelsey tells that "the Spirit" was comparable to that of experiencing an angel and that the two were used interchangeably. "The Spirit" was viewed as a personality, and the individual in contact with "the Spirit" is given wisdom and understanding and power, which the Spirit possesses.

Chapter 18
Night Visions Lead to the Expansion of Christianity

11. Daniel H. Newhall, "Dreams and the Bible", (D. Min. project, San Francisco Theological Seminary, 1980), 90.

12. Navone, "Dreams in the Bible."

13. Ibid.

Chapter 19
Visions of an Exiled Early Christian Leader

14. Frederick van der Meer, *Apocalypse* (Antwerp: Mercatorfonds, 1978), 23.

15. Ibid., 25.

16. Ibid., 24

17. Carl G. Jung, *Spring,*(1960), 131-33. Quoted by Maria F. Mahoney in *The Meaning of Dreams* (New York: The Citadel Press, 1966), 230.

18. Kelsey, *God, Dreams and Revelation*, 98.

PART FOUR: DREAMS AND VISIONS AMONG POST-BIBLICAL JEWS

Chapter 20
Dreams and Later Judaism

1. Jacob Neusner, *Invitation to the Talmud* (San Francisco: Harper & Row Publishers Inc., 1984), xvi.

2. Savary, et. al., *Dreams and Spiritual Growth*, 19.

Notes

3. Edward Hoffman, *The Book of Splendor: Jewish Mysticism and Modern Psychology*, (Boulder, Colorado; Shambhala Publications Inc., 1981), 16.

I am indebted to Edward Hoffman for the information about the Kabbalah and the *Zohar*, although this movement first came to my attention through Kelsey's *God, Dreams and Revelation*. The teachings of the *Zohar* and the Kabbalah are designed to be transmitted only from "one mouth to the next." According to Hoffman, the purpose of the Kabbalists was to enable individuals to rise beyond their misfortune, not to amass a movement (page 12). As with the *Talmud*, the Zohar takes learning, not just reading, so finding *The Book of Splendor* was a happy experience.

4. Ibid., 140.

5. Ibid., 187.

6. Ibid., 152.

7. Ibid., 157.

8. Ibid., 152.

9. Kelsey, *God, Dreams, and Revelation*, 43-44.

10. Hoffman, *The Book of Splendor*, 102.

11. Ibid., 105.

12. Ibid., 106-7.

13. From a television interview of Ingmar Bergman by Lewis Freedman on WNDT-TV in New York City.

Chapter 21
Visitational Dreams among Moroccan Jews in Israel

14. Yoram Bilu and Henry Abramovitch, "In Search of the Saddig: Visitational Dreams Among Moroccan Jews in Israel," *Psychiatry* 48 (February 1985):83-92.

Yoram Bilu, Ph.D., is a lecturer in the departments of psychology and sociology at the Hebrew University of Jerusalem. Henry Abramovitch, Ph.D., is a lecturer in the department of behaviorial science at the Sackler School of Medicine, Tel Aviv University.

Notes

PART FIVE: DREAMS AND VISIONS IN THE EARLY CHURCH

Chapter 22
Dreams Prepare Early Christian Protestors for Martyrdom

1. Rosemary Rader, "The Martyrdom of Perpetua: A Protest Account of Third Century Christianity," *A Lost Tradition: Women Writers of the Early Church* (Washington, D.C.: University Press of America Inc, 1981), 1-32.

   I am indebted to Louis M. Savary, et. al., for recommending this resource in the bibliography of *Dreams and Spiritual Growth*. Notes 2 and 3 in the following chapter are additional pertinent material to which Savary refers in his book on pages 39 and 49.

2. Origen, *Against Celsus*, VI, 21-23.

3. Augustine Fitzgerald, *The Essays and Hymns of Synesius of Cyrene* (London: Oxford, 1930), 345.

Chapter 23
Dreams among Early Church Leaders

4. Kelsey, *God, Dreams and Revelation*, 102-161.

   Most of this information and the direct quotations in this chapter come from Kelsey's research.

5. Savary, et. al., *Dreams and Spiritual Growth*, 43.

PART SIX: DREAMS TODAY

Chapter 24
Our Ordinary Dreams and the Bible

1. Oppenheim, *Interpretation*, (186-7).

2. Ibid.

3. Delaney, *Living With Your Dreams*, 12.

Notes

4. Ibid., 161-5.

5. Savary, et. al., *Dreams and Spiritual Growth*, 165-6.

6. Ibid., 141-2.

7. Ullman, Montague, and Zimmerman, *Working with Dreams* (New York: Dell Publishing Co., 1979), 124-5.

8. Delany, *Living with your Dreams*, 99.

9. James L. Lynch, *The Language of the Heart: The Body's Response to Human Dialogue* (New York: Basic Books Inc., Publishers, 1985), 255.

Chapter 25
Our Extraordinary Dreams

1. Savary, et. al., *Dreams and Spiritual Growth*, 206.

2. P. Erick Craig, Ed.D., is a psychologist in private practice in Worchestor and Cambridge, Massachusetts. This reference is from a speech given at the 1986 annual Association for the Study of Dreams conference in Ottawa, Canada.

3. Kathleen Raine, introduction to Thetis Blacker's *A Pilgrimage of Dreams* (London: Turnstone Books Ltd., 1986), vii.

4. Blacker, *A Pilgrimage of Dreams*, xv.

5. Jean and Wallace Clift, *Symbols of Transformation* (New York: The Crossroad Publishing Company, 1986), 108.
   This book mentions the baptism symbol.

6. Newhall, *Dreams and the Bible*, 189-93.
   Other observations are made about dream interpretation in general, but I have only mentioned those related to imagery.

7. Ibid., 90.

8. Mary Jane Moffat, *In the Midst of Winter* (New York: Random House Inc., 1982), 208.

9. Ibid., 204-7.

10. Savary, et. al., *Dreams and Spiritual Growth*, 207.

CONCLUSION

1. Savary, et. al., *Dreams and Spiritual Growth*, 50-6; and Kelsey, *God, Dreams, and Revelation*, 158-161.

Notes

2. Lynch, *The Language of the Heart,* 232, 233.

3. O'Flaherty, *Dreams, Illusion and Other Realities,* 8, 53-60, 311, 312.

> In general, we mean that reality is what we value, what we care about (page 8).

> It is indeed possible (and necessary) to distinguish between inner reality and outer reality, it is *not* necessary (or, indeed possible) to value one above the other (pages 53-60).

> Some of us mean that reality is what is solid; others mean that reality is what is *not* solid (page 8).

The following is a list of the things the author finds we normally place under the headings of hard and soft:

Hard	Soft
real	illusory
historical	mythical
true	false
awake	asleep
public	private
permanent	transient
present	past/future (memory/prediction)
outside	inside
objective	subjective
sane	insane
rational	emotional
male	female
Western	Eastern
scientific	religious
right	left

4. Kelsey, *God, Dreams, and Revelation,* 79.

5. Robert A. Johnson, *Inner Work* (San Francisco: Harper & Row, Publishers Inc., 1986), 94-6.

Appendix

A Guide to Biblical Dreams and Visions

This list of biblical dreams and visionary experiences has been helpful to me in individual and group Bible study. At the time I began these studies, I found the best resource outside of the Bible to be *God, Dreams, and Revelations* by Morton Kelsey. Later I supplemented my studies with the *Layman's Bible Commentary*. The recently published *Disciples Study Bible* is another helpful source, especially when studying Revelation. Its preface states, "Dreams, visions, angels are listed among the many ways God uses to tell who he is and to reveal his intentions and purpose."

I have used this list with study groups of the Broadway Baptist Church, Fort Worth, Texas; the Nineteenth Avenue Baptist Church, San Francisco, California; and Crescent Hill Baptist Church, Louisville, Kentucky. They were instrumental in its development and contributed to helping others with whom I have shared it.

Appendix

To remain consistent with the scripture quotations used throughout the book, I use quotations from the New International Version.

DREAMS AND VISIONS IN THE HEBREW BIBLE

These references show us what the Bible says about understanding dreams and visions as well as the importance of prophets.

Deuteronomy 13:2 A legal interpretation of a false prophet is made.

Deuteronomy 3:5 Death is the penalty for the prophet who perverts the use of dreams.

Deuteronomy 18:9-14 As in Leviticus 19:20,31, although dreams are not mentioned, pagan diviners who interpret dreams are to be shunned.

Deuteronomy 18:15-18 Foundation for prophecy and the visionary experiences is established. "It is that he may speak the words of the Lord which the Lord gives him."

Deuteronomy 18:20 This is not an injunction against listening to dreams and visions. The injunction is against failure to distinguish the word of the Lord.

Deuteronomy 18:21-22 How shall we know? A prophet had to speak the word of God, which would "come to pass or come true." Even more important, "his prophecies had to lead the people into closer communion with God."

Numbers 2:6 Dreams and visions are acknowledged as among the ways God communicated his messages. In this story of sibling jealousy, the authority of Moses' teachings are challenged. His brother, Aaron, and sister, Miriam, are told that God does communicate through dreams and visions, but that he speaks to Moses directly.

A Guide to Biblical Dreams and Visions

Jeremiah sheds more light on this as he deals with this problem of distinguishing the false prophets and those with genuine prophetic dreams and visions.

Dreams and Visions of the Patriarchs
These are the first dreams recorded in the scriptures.

The Hebrew language makes no clear distinction between dreams and visions. Dreams were the usual way to receive the vision, but their content often broke through into waking moments. When we read "a vision by night," we interpret "by night" to mean "while sleeping"; thus we understand the vision to be a dream.

We often read, "The Lord appeared...," "The Lord said...," "God in a vision...."

> God was seen....A vision experience at a place of worship or a dream may have been meant. The Bible's interest in in the fact that God speaks to people....The how of the experience is often ignored (*Disciples Study Bible,* Genesis 12:1-1 nn.).

Genesis 11:31 Terah went from Ur of Chaldeans to Haran.

Genesis 12 The Lord said to Abram "Go to a land I will show you" and promised him and his offspring a great future, that he might be a blessing. When Abram got to Canaan, the Lord *appeared* to him and said "to your descendants I give this land." This is the first time we see the word "appeared." Abram honors this "appearance" by setting up an altar. Later, in chapter 13, he goes back to this altar and calls on the Lord before permitting Lot to choose which land he wants. This is the background and setting for the first dream in Scripture.

Genesis 15:1-20 Abram has a vision, in which the Lord appears, followed by a dream. In the vision, the Lord promises him an heir and renews the promise of the land of Canaan for his descendants. The dream contains the ritual used in ancient days for agreements, and Abram understood this to mean that

Appendix

God was turning his promise into a covenant—a contract between God and man. Today's Jewish traditions result from this dream and Abram's response to it.

Genesis 16:7-12 Abram's son by Hagar, Sarai's handmaiden, was borne with the help and comfort of an angel who promised that his descendants would become a nation. Today's Arab nation descends from him. We are still living with the results of Abram's and Hagar's response to their dreams and visions.

Genesis 17:1-22 God in a vision changes Abram's name to Abraham and Sarai's to Sarah, renews the covenant, promises a son by Sarah for the next year, and orders circumcision as a way for man to indicate his keeping of the Covenant with God.

Genesis 18 Three angels, who are later described as two men and the Lord, appear to Abraham and Sarah with the promise of a son. They reveal their errand to destroy Sodom because of its wickedness. Abraham intercedes for Lot.

The word *angel* presents a difficulty. In some passages the words *God* and *angel* are used interchangeably. The word *angel* can be used for an ordinary human messenger. A spiritual messenger from God may appear as a visionary experience in a dream or may appear as a concrete, physical being materializing out of a spiritual reality. An angel is the most common vision of all the visions.

Genesis 19 Two angels come to Sodom and urge Lot to leave with his wife and daughter before the city is destroyed.

Genesis 20:1-7 Sarah's identity is revealed to King Abimelech in a clairvoyant dream.

Genesis 22:1-3 The story of Abraham being tested begins with a conversation between God and Abraham. The how of the conversation is not described. "Early in the morning..." (verse 3) may describe a night vision.

Genesis 22:11 The angel calls to Abraham, saving Isaac, Abraham's son by Sarah, from being sacrificed.

Genesis 22:15 The angel calls the second time and renews his promise to multiply Abraham's descendants, adding that all the Nation shall be blessed because of them.

A Guide to Biblical Dreams and Visions

Genesis 26: 1-5, 24-25 The Lord appears to Isaac twice and renews His covenant with him and tells him where to sojourn. When he has trouble with the local people over the water wells, God appears again and reassures him. Isaac builds an altar and peace results.

Genesis 28:10-22 Jacob dreams of a ladder that reaches to heaven with angels going up and coming down. God is standing above it and He renews his Covenant. Jacob anoints the stone pillar he slept on and makes a vow to give a tenth of all he would get; thus, the idea of the tithe was established.

Genesis 31:10 God tells Jacob in a dream to leave his Uncle Laban and return home. In a dream Jacob sees striped-spotted and mottled male goats mate with the flock, and an angel appears and says "I am God of Bethel, where you anointed a pillar and made a vow." The angel tells him to return to the land of his birth. Jacob interprets this to mean he is to take with him the livestock he had gained as wages.

Genesis 31:24 God protects Joseph from Laban's anger by appearing to Laban in "a dream by night."

Genesis 32:2 Jacob is met by an army of angels on his way home.

Genesis 32:24 A man (called *angel* in reference to this experience in Hosea 12:4) wrestles with Jacob all night, leaving Jacob crippled and limping. This happens after Jacob learns that he is to be met by Esau, which suggests a dream dealing with unfinished business. The man (angel) tells Jacob he has striven with God and gives him a new name—Israel. ("Man" may mean "Someone." See *Disciples Study Bible* Genesis 32:24-30 n.)

Note: We have seen the importance of dreams and visions in the lives of the patriarchs. We have seen their acceptance of them as a way of letting God direct their lives; thus evolved the Hebrew theory of dreams and visions: that they are *one medium* of direct contact used by God to give man special knowledge of the world and of himself, and to guide and direct humankind.

Appendix

Dreams during the Time of Judges

From the death of Joshua until the time of Eli and Samuel, approximately 400 years, thirteen judges ruled Israel. During this time we read of angels and signs and learn that dreams are still considered important. Space will not permit our looking at every reference, but through Gideon we get a glimpse of all three.

Samuel is the last of the judges and first of the prophets.

Judges 2:1-3; 13:2-23 God continues to be represented by an angel and to speak through an angel during the time of Judges. We see this in the story of Gideon.

Judges 6:11-22 An angel appears to Gideon while he is beating out wheat in a wine press in order to save it from the Midianites. The Lord calls him to deliver Israel from the hand of Midian. After a dialogue the angel gives him a sign by touching the meat and unleavened bread with his staff and causing fire to spring up from the rock and consume the meat and bread.

Judges 7:13-15 The Lord has told Gideon (in verses 9-11) to spy on the Midianite camp, telling him he will hear something to strengthen him against the Midianites. What he overhears is an enemy soldier telling his dream to a friend and the friend's interpretation of it foreseeing the fall of Midian by the sword of Gideon. Hearing this, Gideon worships God, and with confidence in the outcome sets out to defeat the enemy. This is an example of how God speaks to his people even through the dreams of unbelievers.

1 Samuel 3:1 Near the end of the time of Judges, while Samuel is a young boy and has not yet become a judge, the Bible says "...word from the Lord was rare and visions infrequent." This is perhaps because the Judges and people did not listen to them. We really don't know, but there seems to be a breakdown in communication with God. However, God speaks to the boy Samuel in the night, initiating communication with the Israelites through what we call an *auditory vision*.

A Guide to Biblical Dreams and Visions

1 Samuel 3:3 It is night and Samuel has gone to bed when he hears a voice. Typical of young children, he is not able to distinguish between outer and inner reality, so he runs to Eli, asking him if he called. The third time this happens, Eli tells him to say "Yes, Lord, I am here." So Samuel lies down again and when he hears his name replies as Eli advised. This seems to be an auditory experience, but later it's referred to as a vision. Now God tells Samuel he is ready to fulfill what he has spoken against Eli and his sons. Samuel is afraid to tell Eli at first, but does so the next morning at Eli's insistence. Eli accepts it as being from the Lord.

Samuel grows, and from this experience "all Israel (verse 20) from Dan even to Beersheba knew that Samuel was confirmed as a prophet of the Lord."

After Eli and his sons and house are killed in a battle with the Philistines, Samuel becomes judge and priest and guides Israel through great crises during the Nation's transition into a monarchy. He anoints Israel's first king, Saul.

Dreams during the Time of Kings

> "As the kings of Israel got into more and more trouble, the record of their own dreams ceased" (Kelsey, *God, Dreams, and Revelation*, 28-29).

1 Samuel 28:5-19 Israel's first king, Saul, did not listen to his prophet, Samuel. When Samuel died, Saul found himself in great distress, feeling alone and realizing he had lost his guidance. He saw his enemies come upon him. He called on the Lord, but the Lord did not answer by dreams, by Urim, nor by prophets (1 Samuel 28:6). He was so distraught he broke his own law and called on a medium. When Samuel appeared (this was a visionary experience since Samuel was dead) and asked why he was being summoned, Saul admitted, "God has departed from me and answers me no more, either through prophets or by dreams." This tells us that dreams were greatly valued.

Appendix

Note: Israel apparently believed contact with dead spirits might be possible, but it was absolutely wrong to do so. Yet Saul is so distressed when he tries to seek God's guidance and fails that he resorts to this practice of Israel's neighbors. "...why God allowed it to work in this instance the Bible does not say," but we know he uses it for the purpose of notifying Saul of the punishment he faced. (See *Disciples Bible Study* 1 Samuel 28:15-18 n.)

2 Samuel 7:4-17 After Saul comes the great King David and his prophet Nathan. The Lord (2 Samuel 74; 1 Chronicles 17:3) in a vision (2 Samuel 7:17) to Nathan at night, tells him to instruct David not to build the temple but to leave it for his descendants to build. David himself sees the angel of the Lord, who gives him a chance to repent (2 Samuel 24:16 and 1 Chronicles 21:15).

1 Kings 3:5-15 Solomon's source of wisdom appears to be the dream (1 Kings 3:5-15): "...the Lord appeared to Solomon in a dream by night; and God said 'Ask what I shall give you.'" Verse 15 says, "And Solomon awoke, and behold, it was a dream." If you don't value dreams, you might be inclined to say that by the way Solomon behaved, it must have been "only" a dream. However, if you read further, you will see that Solomon interprets this as being God's way of speaking. He goes to Jerusalem, stands before the ark of the covenant, offers burnt offerings and peace offerings, and makes a feast for his servants.

1 Kings 9:2 God appears to Solomon a second time, after he has finished building the temple. The Bible describes the appearance "as he had appeared to him at Gibeon" (1 Kings 9:2), so we know it must have been in a dream again.

2 Kings 1:15; 2 Kings 2:11-13 As Israel continues in Kings, the kings seemed to less and less follow God's guidance through dreams or prophets of God, and we have no record of their dreams. Instead God spoke to Israel through Elijah and Elisha. Marvelous things happened, and at the end of his life (2 Kings 2:11), Elijah was taken up by a whirlwind in chariots of fire with horses. Elisha was with him and saw this happen; he caught Elijah's mantle and in so doing fell heir to the same spirit and power that had been Elijah's. Wonderful things continued in Elisha's life. After his death, one more experience is recorded in the historical part of the Hebrew Bible: the angel of the Lord destroyed Sennacherib's famous army before Jerusalem (2 Kings 19:35; Isaiah 37:36).

Dreams and the Prophets

From the following we can see why the prophets were called seers.

Jeremiah 1:11a And the word of the Lord came to me saying "Jeremiah, what do you see?"

Ezekiel 1:1 "I saw visions..."

Amos 1:1 words of Amos...which he saw

Micah 1:1 and 3:6 The word of the Lord that came to Micah...the vision he saw...

Isaiah 3:1 This is what Isaiah son of Amoz saw...

Isaiah 6:1 ...I saw the Lord seated on a throne...

Nahum 1:1 The book of the vision of Nahum

Habakkuk 1:1 The oracle of God that Habakkuk, the prophet, saw.

Zechariah 1:7-8 Zechariah said "I saw in the night..."

FOR FURTHER STUDY:

Not all of the prophets *saw* visions. In Zephaniah, we read "The word of the Lord which came to Zephaniah..." (1:1).

What is meant by the word *vision*? *saw* and *see*? Does "visions" mean the content of a dream and a spontaneous intrusion on the consciousness from the non-physical or spiritual realm? Or intuitive insight from the available facts presented to the people in the form of a vision as may be the case in Zechariah's series of eight visions?

Appendix

A study of their content provides clues to some degree. *The Layman's Bible Commentary* 15, page 96, discusses this, saying:

> For the early prophets a glimpse of some object or setting provided the occasion and stimulus from God: a momentary experience triggered the process of insight in the mind of the prophet so that what occurred had the intensity of a "vision" and became organized around certain vividly sensed words which were recognized as having the force of the word of the Lord.

Kelsey, in *God, Dreams, and Revelation,* uses the term "direct confrontation of God himself" as a source of the prophets' messages, whether the prophets see God or speak as God's mouthpiece. He reminds us that psychologically there is little difference between having our vision possessed by images or having our vocal apparatus possessed, resulting in speech. However the prophets received their messages, the dreams/visions clearly come from outside this "space-time continuum we call history." The prophets seemed to be in contact with both physical and non-physical realities. The prophets' very approach to life was born out of their experiences with the non-physical. The images they saw were not so important as their ability to see their significance and speak about it (spiritual discernment).

How Do You Tell The Real Thing?

Jeremiah especially deals with this. A major problem of the prophets is distinguishing between the false prophets and the genuine prophetic dream and vision.

Jeremiah 1:11 Jeremiah saw an almond tree. The Hebrew word for almond means "early awake." The almond tree is the first tree to bud and announce approaching spring. Jeremiah understood this to mean that he was like the almond tree—early awake—quick to see the significance of what he saw and to announce it.

A Guide to Biblical Dreams and Visions

Jeremiah 1:13 He saw a "boiling pot" facing south or from the north. He understood this to symbolize the fermentation taking place in the north that would result in Judah being invaded. The covenant people were worshipping idols made by their own hands, and Jeremiah was being called through these visions to remind the people of God's covenant and their part of the covenant, which they weren't keeping.

Jeremiah 14:14 By this time the king and queen mother and 10,000 people were taken captive by Nebuchadnezzar (II Kings 24:8-17). This chapter opens with a severe drought, and the people are mourning and pleading with God to remember they are his people. This verse is part of a dialogue between Jeremiah and God, in which God says he can't accept his people on their shallow pretenses of turning to him. Jeremiah tells God that the prophet has told them there is no danger. God says these prophets are prophesying false visions and the deceit of their own minds.

Jeremiah 23:16-22 Through Jeremiah God describes the ungodliness of the prophets and warns against prophets who "speak visions of their own minds, not from the mouth of the Lord." "Of their own minds" may refer to their own dreams instead of prophetic dreams or visions, or maybe it means made-up dreams or wishful thinking. Whatever it means, they were giving the people false hope that all would be all right no matter what they did.

Had they really received messages from a higher source than themselves, they would have perceived and proclaimed God's word and not their own and would have turned the people from evil. Claiming to have a higher source for their messages when they had none, they "emptied a true vehicle of divine communication of its significance (Numbers 12:6)."

Jeremiah 23:23-24 God is not limited. It is reasonable to apply this passage to our consciousness and unconsciousness. God surely is not limited to just the conscious moments of our existence.

Appendix

Jeremiah 23:25 God knew about the prophets who said "I have dreamed" and who pretended to have authentic revelation from God. *The Layman's Bible Commentary* 12, page 73, takes the position that Jeremiah did not mean to discount dreaming as one authentic mode of prophetic revelation.

Jeremiah 23:27; 23:28 "...the dreams they tell one another..." and "Let the prophet who has a dream tell his dream, but let the one who has my word speak it faithfully" makes a distinction between dreams that deal with their personal lives and those that deal with a prophetic message.

Jeremiah 23:29 "An authentic revelation is known by its effects, a fire consumes what it touches. A hammer-blow breaks rocks. So too God's word is known by what it does" (*The Layman's Bible Commentary* 12, 73).

Jeremiah 27:16 "Do not listen to your prophets [your diviners, your dreamers, your soothsayers, or your sorcerers,]...They are prophesying lies to you..."

Jeremiah 28:9 Jeremiah's only solution to the problem of distinguishing between the different kinds of dreams and the false prophet from God's prophet is that "time would tell whose prophecy was true." This reminds us of what we read in Deuteronomy about waiting to see if the interpretation came true.

Jeremiah 29:8 "Do not let your prophets and your diviners who are among you deceive you. Do not listen to the dreams which they encourage you to have." The Hebrew people continued to look to false prophets and diviners who tried to create revelation instead of depending on God for it.

Jeremiah 31:26 "At this I awoke and looked around. My sleep had been pleasant to me." This indicates Jeremiah had been dreaming and refers to the encouraging character of the preceding vision (*The Layman's Bible Commentary* 12, 92). In this vision, God gives hope for the future. Again we need to remember that dreams were regarded as authentic means of divine communication, and that Jeremiah has not been against

A Guide to Biblical Dreams and Visions

dreams but the way they were being used. Jeremiah's value of dreams and visions is found in Lamentations 2:9, wherein he laments that visions no longer come to the prophet.

Dreams in the Poetic Writings

The Writings are the parts of the Hebrew Bible that are neither law, history, nor prophecy. Psalm, Job, and Daniel contain many passages about dreams and visions. Ecclesiastes, Song of Solomon, and Lamentations are also considered Writings and mention dreams.

Ecclesiastes 5:3 "As a dream comes when there are so many cares..."
Ecclesiastes 5:7 "Much dreaming and many words are meaningless." These two references express the only negative attitude about dreams in the scriptures. Remember, this book is written by a skeptical person. Also, it speaks of humans relating to God rather than God's communicating and breaking through to people.
The Song of Solomon 3:1-4 and 5:2-8 The maiden tells two dreams in which she searches for her beloved. These are beautiful examples that deal with personal concerns. The fact that they are included indicates that the Bible values this level of dream life also.
Lamentations 2:9 Again we have distress expressed over visions no longer coming to the prophet. This is one of the desolations lamented by the prophet.

Daniel

*Because of its prophetic themes, this book might be considered with the prophets; however, the Hebrew Bible places it among the Writings, and if we take a look into Ezekiel we find Daniel considered more a pious sage. He is described in **Ezekiel 14:4,20** as righteous, in **Ezekiel 28:3**, wise. Although he was a seer, he was not a preacher of righteousness by*

Appendix

vocation. He was more of a statesman holding a high office in the government that held him captive, thus an example of God's revelation of special information through a lay person.

Daniel 1:17; 2:1 Again dreams and visions are equated. Daniel's wisdom is tied to the fact that he can interpret dreams and visions. We realize from this introduction that the whole book concerns itself with dreams and visions.

Daniel 2: The whole chapter deals with Nebuchadnezzar's troubling dream, which he orders his court sages to recall and interpret or be destroyed. After Daniel and his three friends pray, Daniel receives a vision of the dream and interprets it. The king acknowledges Daniel's God and makes Daniel ruler over the province of Babylon and chief of all the wise men.

Daniel 2:25-28 "Magicians and diviners cannot interpret dreams correctly. Only the true God can give the revelation necessary to interpret dreams. Dreams were perceived by ancients to be an approach that divine beings used to reveal themselves to humans. The king's dreams revealed God's coming active in history" (*Disciples Study Bible*, n.).

Daniel 2:44-45 Besides establishing the superiority of divinely inspired wisdom over human wisdom, this part of the king's dreams gives a vision of a new and everlasting kingdom set up by the Ancient of Days. Daniel also has this vision in **7:13-14.**

Daniel 3:28 Daniel's three friends are delivered by an angel from the fiery furnace, by which they were being punished for refusing to bow to golden images. This resulted in the king's decree of death for any who speak against the God of the Israelites.

Daniel 4 Nebuchadnezzar's tree dream predicts his insanity. None of his wise men can interpret this dream. Daniel explained that the tree symbolized the king who was about to lose his reason and become like a beast and eat grass in the wasteland. The dream is fulfilled and King Nebuchadnezzar is restored when he acknowledges God as the one God whose dominion is heaven and earth and lives forever.

A Guide to Biblical Dreams and Visions

Daniel 5:5 Handwriting on the wall, which is a *group vision*, is interpreted by Daniel to mean the Babylonian kingdom is at an end. That night Babylon is invaded and the king is killed.

Daniel 6:22-23,26 Daniel is delivered by an angel from the lions. He had been trapped by those jealous of his position. This resulted in the accusers and their families being thrown to the lions and devoured. Everyone was commanded to "fear and reverence before the God of Daniel" (verse 26).

Daniel 7-12: Daniel dreams of four beasts (chapter 7), the ram and he-goat (chapter 8), seventy weeks (chapter 9), and an angel by the river (chapters 10-12).

Note the content of the following verses in chapters 7-12:

Daniel 7:13-14 A new and everlasting kingdom set up by the Ancient of Days

Daniel 9:21-22 Gabriel came to Daniel while he was praying (Daniel prayed before interpreting the king's dream) to give him wisdom and understanding.

Daniel 10:5 Vision of angel by the river that Daniel alone saw. Daniel describes how terrified he felt—he was comforted by the angel and learns from the angel that men of violence will fail to fulfill vision **(11:14)** and about individual resurrection of the dead **(12:2-10,)** the only place in the Hebrew Bible where the term "everlasting life" is used).

How Daniel describes these experiences and his responses is worth noting:

Daniel 4:13 "In the vision I saw while lying in my bed..."

Daniel 7:1 "Daniel had a dream, and visions passed through his mind as he was lying on his bed. He wrote down the substance of his dream."

Daniel 10:16b "I am overcome with anguish because of my vision, my Lord, and I am helpless."

Appendix

Job

In this drama of the Inner Life, we can expect to find dreams and visions. Job and each of his three friends clearly express what can occur in dreams.

1. Dreams frighten.

Job 7:13-14 Job has a nightmare, which he blames on God, complaining, "You frighten me with dreams and terrify me with visions."

Job 4:13-14 Eliphay knew the fear of "disquieting dreams of the night."

2. Dreams fade away easily.

Job 20:5-9 Zapher compared the wicked to dreams and visions, saying the wicked would disappear like dreams and visions in the night.

3. Dreams warn and are a means of preparing people to hear God's message.

Job 33:15-16 Elihu gives the most important message about dreams. He says God's purpose in terrifying people in dreams with warnings is to lead them back to Him—to bring about conversion— turn from evil, to redeem, to save. *The Layman's Bible Commentary* 8 calls this "divine speaking." Dreams and visions are a means of direct communication with God. Job talks to God about even his dreams. Note that Elihu is not declaring suffering itself a means of God speaking, but a means of preparing people to hear God's message.

Notes in *Disciples Study Bible* points out that Job's friends know the nature of revelation. They did not know Job's situation and had yet to deal with God's using events he had not directly caused as instruments of revelation.

A Guide to Biblical Dreams and Visions

Psalms

Throughout Psalms there are references to angels and messengers of God. No clear distinction is made between sleep and wakefulness. We conclude from references that in the nighttime something came through to the psalmist that he thought of as being from God.

Psalm 22:2; 32:4 References to disturbing nights

Psalm 42:6 The psalmist says, "His song is with me in the night..." Whether God's song comes to him in a dream or while awake during a sleepless night we don't know, but either is possible.

Psalm 63:6-8 Communion with God in the night

Psalm 73:20 A nightmare from which one awakens despising the image of wickedness.

Psalm 89:19-37 Psalmists sing of God speaking in a vision.

Psalm 73:20 A nightmare from which one awakened despising the image of wickedness.

Psalm 126:1 Dreams are likened to the wish that has been fulfilled.

Psalm 127:2 The Lord "grants sleep to those he loves," which cannot be had simply by rising early and working late.

DREAMS AND VISIONS IN THE NEW TESTAMENT

Reverence for dreams and visions continued during the time of Jewish history between the Hebrew Bible and the New Testament. The writings of that time, called the Apocrypha, deal with dreams in the spirit of Job and Daniel.

Since the Greek culture was flourishing at the time of Jesus' birth, it will help us to understand the Grecian attitude toward dreams.

Appendix

Greek literature indicates that they valued dreams as much as the Hebrews did. They treated dreams with reverence, believing they were intrusions of a non-human or more-than-human source, communication from the divine. One difference is that they did not evaluate them as critically as the Hebrews did. This seems strange, considering the Greeks' emphasis on rational understanding. However, a closer look reveals that the Greeks considered the irrational aspects of life as much a reality as the rational.

The Greek language had twelve different ways of describing a confrontation with the spiritual world or an intrusion from the non-physical. Kelsey discusses these words in *God, Dreams, and Revelation*. The *Disciples Study Bible* provides notes discussing the experiences in which these are used under the main topic "Revelation."

The Greeks had two words for dreams, three for visions, and other words for the following non-physical perceptions:

ecstasy or *trance* — refer to either sleeping **(Acts 10:10; 11:15)** or waking **(Mark 5:42 and 15:1; Luke 5:26)** experiences and those which occur on the edge of wakefulness while going to sleep or waking up **(Acts 22:17,** may have been Paul's state when he was praying in the temple and saw the Lord speak).

to become in Spirit — a state in which one could see visions and be informed or spoken to directly by the spirit **(Revelation 1:10).**

to stand by — refers to such realities as the Lord, an angel, a man **(Luke 1:11; Acts 10:30,16:9,23:11,27:23).**

angel — a divine being sent by God; such a being is without physical reality but is still powerful, very real, and significant.

demons and the devil (Satan) — realities without physical bodies, believed to be able to possess a human person's body or psyche. Jesus spoke with demons **(Matthew 8:31; Mark 5:9; Luke 8:31)** and was tempted by Satan after his baptism.

disclosure of revelation — uncovering what was formerly hidden in the realm of spirit **(Romans 16:25; 1 Corinthians 14:6 and 26; 2 Corinthians 12:1 and 7; Galatians 2:2)**. In 2 Corinthians the Greek word for disclosure of revelation is linked closely with visions.

seeing — the vision **(Mark 9:9; Luke 9:36; Revelation 1:11, 1:12)** Visionary contents were included in seeing along with seeing the outer, physical world.

The Gospels

Jesus' Birth

Dreams and visions enable the infant Jesus to survive and describe experiences of non-human intervention on behalf of his birth.

Luke 1:11-22 The angel Gabriel announces the birth of John the Baptist.

Luke 1:26-38 The angel Gabriel tells Mary she is to be the mother of the Son of God and she is to call him Jesus.

Luke 1:38-45 Elizabeth receives the information by the Spirit.

Matthew 1:20 An angel in a dream appears to Joseph and reveals the identity of the child Mary is to have.

Luke 2:9,13 A vision of an angel and a multitude of angels appears to shepherds announcing the birth of Jesus.

Matthew 2:12 The wise men are warned in a dream to avoid Herod.

Appendix

Matthew 2:13 An angel warns Joseph to flee with Jesus and Mary to Egypt.

Matthew 2:19-23 An angel informs Joseph of Herod's death and instructs Joseph not to go into Judea because Herod's son rules there.

Luke 2:21 Jesus is circumcised after eight days. He is called Jesus, the name the angel gave him before his conception.

Jesus' Life

There is no record of Jesus' dreams, but visionary experiences surround all the important experiences of his life.

Baptism by John the Baptist:
Matthew 3:16; Mark 1:9-11; Luke 3:21-22; John 1:29-34 The Spirit in the appearance of a dove descends upon Jesus and a voice from heaven is heard by those present (a group vision).

Temptation in the wilderness:
Matthew 4:1, 4:3, 4:11; Mark 1:12, 1:13; Luke 4:1 Jesus is driven "by the Spirit"—a state in which one sees visions and is informed or spoken to directly by the Spirit.

The tempter comes (a visionary experience in an encounter with the primary source of evil).

Jesus is ministered to and restored by angels.

Casting out demons and evil spirits:
Matthew 8:28-32; Mark 1:24-26 and 34, 3:11, 5:12-13; Luke 4:33-35 Jesus indicated he recognized realities without physical bodies who could possess a human person and cause him/her to be troubled. There are twenty-seven such stories in the gospels. None describe seeing demons or evil spirits, but there are some auditory visions in which Jesus spoke with demons and evil spirits.

Jesus allowed demons to enter into a herd of swine.

Jesus rebuked demons for trying to reveal his identity.

Teachings show he believed in angels or the reality of non- material beings that were good:

John 1:51 He gave Nathanael expectation of seeing angels.

Matthew 18:10 He taught that angels of children behold the face of the Father in heaven.

Luke 16:22 He said that Lazarus was carried to Abraham's bosom by angels.

Matthew 22:30; Mark 12:25; Luke 20:36 He compared men in resurrected life to angels in his explanation that men do not marry after death.

Matthew 16:27; 24:31,36; Mark 8:38 He explained that when he returned to earth, the angels would be with him, even though the angels did not know when this time would be.

Matthew 13:49; Mark 13:27; Luke 12:9, 15:10, 12:9 He taught through parables and direct statement that angels would gather the chosen of God.

Matthew 13:39, 25:31, 41 He contrasted angels with the devil and "his angels."

Matthew 26:53 When he told his disciple to put away his sword, he revealed that angels had power against the destructive powers.

Obviously Jesus accepted the existence of a spiritual realm and its power to affect the physical realm. We should expect Jesus, as the Son of God, to have knowledge about all reality. We accept it when he speaks of flowers and other things from the physical world in his parables, but tend to overlook that he deals with angels, demons, and the transformation of the body.

Jesus' Transfiguration

Matthew 17:1-5: Mark 9:2-4; Luke 9:28-35 Moses and Elijah appear and Jesus is filled with radiant light (group vision ecstasy)

Luke 22:43 Jesus is strengthened by an angel as he experiences agony after the transfiguration.

Appendix

Jesus' Death

John 12:27-33 Jesus' death is foretold by a voice from heaven in answer to his prayer, "Father, glorify Thy name."

Matthew 27:19 Pilot is warned through his wife's dream of Jesus' righteousness and that he should have nothing to do with him.

Jesus' Resurrection

"In His resurrection body Jesus clearly transcended time and space. He had power to vanish so as to cease to be seen by others" and to reappear, helping the disciples to understand who he was. Without the resurrection Jesus would have been no more than a prophet who had failed to fulfill their hopes for a messiah (Disciples Study Bible).

The resurrection itself is a breakthrough of the spiritual world into the physical, taking power out of death and giving evidence of life after death.

Matthew 28:2; Mark 16:5; Luke 24:4; John 20:12 All resurrection accounts speak of angels.

Luke 24:23 This vision of angels is described to Jesus by two disciples on the road to Emmaus before they recognize him.

Summary of Dreams in the Gospels

From the gospels we learn that the earliest followers of Jesus:

1. accepted that the meaning and purpose of the outer world originated in the inner spiritual world;

2. accepted that God speaks and works through this world of dreams, trance and vision, and appearances of angels; and

3. viewed both the physical and non-physical worlds as necessary to people. Without the record of these encounters with the non- physical reality, the meaning of the New Testa-

ment and the gospels would be difficult to understand. They provide further proof and understanding of this invisible world of dreams and vision.

The Apostles and Dreams

Through powerful dreams and visions, the Bible tells us how God revealed himself to his chosen people (those He has chosen to be his servants and through them bless all people). This continues now through the Apostles, who were chosen by Jesus to establish his church. Dreams, visions, and angels continue to mark every major event during the time of the Apostles, indicating their importance in the communication between God and humankind.

Acts 1:10-11 Two men in white (angels) appear after Jesus ascends into a cloud and promises Jesus will return.

Acts 2:1-4 The followers of Jesus heard a sound like the blowing violent wind and saw what seemed to be tongues of fire; and began to speak languages they had not studied with the revelation of the Holy Spirit on the Day of Pentecost. The wind and fire remind us of Exodus, wherein we see objects in the physical world used in an unusual way, which gives them a visionary quality. The word for *wind* and *spirit* is the same in the Hebrew language. The spirit, like the wind, is uncontrollable, mysterious, powerful, and can only be seen in what it does. Besides being like the wind, the spirit is like a flame, which cleanses and consumes and is awesome and dangerous. These experiences were a breakthrough of the non-physical (spiritual) reality into the physical and conscious. They exposed the apostles to new experiences and to new understanding of dreams and visions.

Acts 2:16-18 Peter quotes from Joel 2:28, applying his prophesy to the revelation of Spirit on the day of Pentecost.

Appendix

Acts 5:19, 12:7-16 Twice an angel rescues the Apostles from prison by not only appearing visually but also acting in a physical sense by opening doors and waking Peter.

Acts 7:30, 35, 38, 53 Stephen recites the history of the angel who made Moses their deliverer and gave Moses the divine law.

Acts 7:55-8:1 Stephen sees a heavenly vision of the glory of God and Jesus as he faces death by stoning.

Acts 8:26-40 Philip experiences the interchangeability of angels with the spirit. Luke considers angels essentially the same as promptings from the Spirit and thus uses them interchangeably.

Acts 9:3 Saul is converted on his way to Damascus by a blinding light from which he hears the voice of Jesus.

Acts 9:10-12 Ananias is instructed in a vision to go to Paul, who in prayer sees a vision of Ananias coming to him and healing his sight.

Acts 10 Peter has a dream-trance in which God shows him through symbols that it was right to bring Gentiles into the early Christian Church. At the same time, Cornelius, a Gentile, has a vision of an angel while he is praying. The angel tells him to send for Peter, who is in the next town. Before Cornelius' men can knock, Peter is informed by the Spirit (an example of Spirit and angel being interchangeable) that they are outside, and he goes to them immediately.

Acts 11:1-18 Dreams and visions are given by Peter to the Christians at Jerusalem. They had previously attacked Peter for accepting Cornelius and his household. Peter cites the dreams and visions as the reasons for what he did, and they not only accepted this as right but glorified God too.

Acts 11:28 The Spirit inspired the first missionary project: a contribution by the Christians at Antioch to those in Judea for relief from the famine.

Acts 12:23 An angel brings God's judgment on King Herod. He had been attacking the Christians and allowing himself to be praised as God without giving credit to God.

Acts 13:2 The Holy Spirit instructed the Christians at Antioch to set apart Paul and Barnabas "for the work to which he was calling them."

Acts 16:6 Paul has a vision in the night of a man of Macedonia begging him to "come over to Macedonia and help us." Paul interprets it and acts upon it, and as a result Christianity came to the West instead of into Asia.

Acts 18:9 God spoke to Paul one night in a vision. He had come to Corinth and was discouraged, but as the result of this visionary promise and his response to it, Paul stayed in Corinth one-and-a- half years, working, preaching and writing letters. Two thirds of the letters he left us were written there.

Acts 19:21, 20:22-23, 21:4, 22:17 Paul had difficulty with his decision to go to Jerusalem, which he thought was of the Spirit's leading. He went and was arrested.

Acts 23:11 "The following night the Lord stood near Paul" in prison and directed him to go to Rome.

Acts 27:23-24 In a storm at sea, an angel assures Paul in the night that he and all on the ship will reach Rome safely.

1 Corinthians 9:1, 15:8; 2 Corinthians 12:1-7; Galatians 1:11-16 In his letters Paul makes some references about himself and his visions. He makes clear that the knowledge and insight he is discussing is imparted directly from God, and he shows that this makes a real difference in peoples' outer life. His view of these experiences, then, is that he has been given insight into the world of the spirit and, through this insight, guidance in the outer world.

1 Corinthians 9:1 Paul says, "Have I not seen Jesus our Lord?" He is no doubt referring to visions of the risen Lord.

1 Corinthians 15:8 "...he (Jesus) appeared to...and least of all he appeared to me."

2 Corinthians 12:1-5 and 7 Using third person, Paul mentions visions of paradise. He isn't certain how he received this vision, nor does he say what paradise is like, other than to say he heard inexpressible things. We understand this in the context of Paul's suffering.

Appendix

Note that he relates this experience to show that his personal faith was strengthened by a vision. He didn't gain anything from the vision itself, nor from the way he experienced it, nor from its contents. Experiencing a vision doesn't mean that he is more favored. Paul doesn't say other Christians should expect to have similar visions. A full discussion of this passage can be found in the *Disciples Bible Study*.

Galatians 1:11-17 "...the gospel I preached, I received it by revelation from Jesus Christ." Not only was Paul's life transformed by his vision of Jesus, but the message he preached was revealed through visionary experiences.

Revelation On the Island of Patmos, John writes all of this book, and he describes the experience as being "carried away in the Spirit" and simply seeing and hearing visionary beings who spoke and moved as in a dream. John had this extraordinary spiritual experience when he was worshiping on the first day of the week, a time Christians celebrated Christ's resurrection. It "came through visions, trances, and through spiritual, and not unconscious communion with God—the highest form of inspiration" (Charles, *A Critical History of the Doctrine of a Future Life*).

Bibliography

BIBLES

Holman Bible Publishers. *Disciples Study Bible*. Nashville: Holman Bible Publishers, 1988.

------. *Williams New Testament.*. Nashville: Holman Bible Publishers, 1986.

International Bible Society. *The Holy Bible, New International Version*. Grand Rapids, MI: Zondervan Publishing House, 1984.

Sandmel, Samuel, ed. *The New English Bible with the Apocrypha,* Oxford Study Edition. New York: Oxford University Press, 1976.

William Collins Sons & Co., Ltd. *Fount Children's Bible*. London: Fount Paperbacks, 1981.

BIBLE COMMENTARIES

Kelly, Balmer H. "Ezra, Nehemiah, Esther, Job." *The Layman's Biblical Commentary* 8. Richmond, VA: The John Knox Press, 1960.

Krist, Howard L. "Jeremiah, Lamentations." *The Layman's Biblical Commentary* 12. Richmond, VA: The John Knox Press, 1960.

Gailey, James H. "Micah, Nahum, Habakkuk, Zephaniah, Haggai, Zechariah, Malachi." *The Layman's Biblical Commentary* 15. Richmond, VA: The John Knox Press, 1960.

Bibliography

BOOKS

Blacker, Thetis. *A Pilgrimage of Dreams*. London: Turnstone Ltd., 1986.

Charles, R. H. *A Critical History of the Doctrine of a Future Life*. 2d ed., rev. and enl. London: Adam and Charles Black, 1913.

Clift, Jean and Wallace. *Symbols of Transformation*. New York: Crossroad, 1986.

Delaney, Gayle. *Living Your Dreams*. Rev. ed. San Francisco: Harper & Row, 1988.

Gnuse, Robert Karl. *The Dream Theophany of Samuel*. Lanham, Maryland: University of America, Inc., 1984.

Hoffman, Edward. Chapter 6 in *The Way of Splendor: Jewish Mysticism and Modern Psychology*. Boston: Shambhala Publications, Inc., 1981.

Johnson, Robert A. *Inner Work*. San Francisco: Harper & Row, 1986.

Kelsey, Morton. *God, Dreams and Revelation*. Minneapolis: Augsburg Press, 1974.

------. *Dreams: A Way to Listen to God*. New York: Paulist Press, 1978.

Lynch, James L. *The Language of the Heart: The Bodys' Response to Human Dialogue*. New York: Basic Book Publishers, Inc., 1985.

Moffat, Mary Jane. *In the Midst of Winter*. New York: Random House, Inc., 1982.

Neusner, Jacob. *Invitation to the Talmud*. San Francisco: Harper & Row, Publishers Inc., 1984.

O'Flaherty, Wendy Doniger. *Dreams, Illusions and Other Realities*. Chicago: The University of Chicago Press, 1984.

Oppenheim, A. Leo. "Interpretation of Dreams in the Ancient Near East," *Transactions of the American Philosophical Society*. Philadelphia: American Philosophical Society, 1956.

Peck, M. Scott. *People of the Lie*. New York: Simon and Schuster, 1983.

Reader's Digest Association, Inc. *Great People of the Bible*. Pleasantville, New York: Reader's Digest Association, Inc., 1974.

Reed, Henry. *Getting Help from Your Dreams*. Virginia Beach: Inner Vision Publishing Co., 1985.

Savary, Louis M., Patricia H. Berne, and Strephon Kaplan Williams. *Dreams and Spiritual Growth*. New York: Paulist Press, 1984.

Self, William, and Carolyn Shealy. *Confessions of a Nomad*. Atlanta: Preachtree Publishers, Ltd., 1983.

Taylor, Jeremy. *Dream Work*. New York: Paulist Press, 1983.

Trawich, Buckner B. *The Bible as Literature*. New York: Barnes & Noble, Inc., 1973.

Ullman, Montague, and Nan Zimmerman. *Working with Dreams*. New York: Dell Publishing Co., 1979.

Van der Meer, Frederick. *Apocalypse*. Antwerp: Mercatorfonds, 1978.

Wilson-Kastner, Patricia, et al. *A Lost Tradition: Women Writers of the Early Church*. Washington, D.C., University Press of America, 1981.

ARTICLES

Bilu, Yoram, and Henry Abramovitch. "Visitational Dreams Among Moroccan Jews in Israel." *Psychiatry* 48(1981): 135-149.

Craig, P. Erik. "Existential View of the Elegant Dream." *Association for the Study of Dreams Newsletter* 3, no. 2 (June 1986):13-4.

Kracke, Waud H. "Cultural and Personal Meanings of Dreams." *Association for the Study of Dreams Newsletter* 3, no. 2 (June 1986):3-4.

Navone, John. "Dreams in the Bible." *The Bible Today*, no. 80 (November 1975):515-8.

Putscher, Marielene. "Dreams and Dream Interpretation in the Bible." *Journal of Psychiatry and Related Science* 19, no. 2 (1982): 144-5.

Siegel, Alan B. "Dream Quest: A Wilderness Ritual." *Association for the Study of Dreams Newsletter*, 2, no. 3 (September 1985):1-5.

UNPUBLISHED DOCUMENTS

McEntire, Dennis P. "The Dream as a Literary Unit," Th.M. thesis, Louisville, KY: Southern Baptist Theological Seminary, 1970.

Bibliography

Meiburg, Albert L. "An Understanding of the Dream as a Means of Divine Revelation," Ph.D. diss., Louisville, KY: Southern Baptist Theological Seminary, 1954.

Newhall, Daniel H. "Dreams and the Bible," D.Min. diss., San Anselmo: San Francisco Theological Seminary, 1980.

SUGGESTED READING

Brown, Eugene M., ed. *Dreams, Visions, and Prophecies of Don Bosco.* New Rochelle: Don Bosco Publications, 1986.

Gendlin, Eugene. *Let Your Body Interpret Your Dreams.* Wilmette: Chiron Publications, 1986.

Evans, Christopher. *Landscapes of the Night.* New York: The Viking Press, 1983.

McDonald, Phoebe. *Dreams: Night Language of the Soul.* New York: The Continuum Publishing Company, 1987.

Riffel, Herman. *Your Dreams: God's Neglected Gift.* New York: Ballantine Books, 1981.

Sanford, John. *Dreams: God's Forgotten Language.* Philadelphia: J. B. Lippincott Company, 1986.

Index

-A-

Abimelech 13-4, 152
Abraham 4-5, 9-10, 13-15, 152
accordian folder image 158
airplane image ix
Ancient Near East 3, 5, 56, 63
   dream practices of 1-3
angel(s) 64, 82, 88, 96, 195
   appear to Joseph (NT) 83-5
   appears to Paul 98
   Gabriel 36
   in Daniel's vision 37
   in Jacob's dream 17-21, 93
   in Revelation 103, 105-6,
   in Saturus' dream vision 134
   Michael 37, 102
   prince of Persia 37
   seraphim 61
   seraphs 59, 61
   Uriel 70
anger 155, 166-7
animal images 35, 133, 172 *See also* creature images.
   bear 35, 136
   cat/kitten 156, 162, 195
   dog 162
   eagle 70-1
   four-footed 91
   goat 20-1, 36, 159
   horse(s) 103
   lion 35, 71, 102, 124, 165
   rabbit 176-7
   ram 36
   sheep, 87-8
animal sacrifice 10
apocalypse 34, 106
apocrypha 69, 77
apron image 158
assurance, dreams provide 10, 21, 25, 65, 84, 97, 107, 112, 136
audition/auditory dreams 48
Augustine 137, 144-5
Athanasius 142

-B-

Baal 5, 40, 50
Babylonia 4, 29, 30, 34, 74
Balaam 43
balancing function of dreams 158, 194
baptism images 179-82
Basil the Great 143-4
bear image 35, 136

Index

beast images 34, 35, 71, 132 *See* animal images *and* creature images.
Belteshazzer 31-2, 34
Bergman, Ingmar 120
biblical symbols and images, study of 182-3
biblical images *See also* animal images, creature images *and* angels.
  barley bread 45
  birds 27, 107, 1179
  bush on fire 39
  City of God 105
  earthquake 104
  elders, twenty-four 102-3
  fire 10, 35, 76
  grain 24, 27
  hired man 88
  ladder 17-9, 93
  lamps, seven flaming 102
  lampstands, seven golden 101
  Male Child 104
  measuring rod, golden 105
  moon 25, 104
  New City 105
  New Jerusalem 105
  rider on white horse 104
  river 73-4, 105
  rock 29
  saints 35
  scroll with seven seals 103
  sea 72, 102
  stars 25, 37, 101, 104, 106
  statue 29
  storm 72
  sun 25, 72, 74, 104
  throne 35, 59, 61
  tree 31-2, 119
  vine 26
  wings 70-1
  woman in purple and scarlet 104
  Woman, The 102

bird image 27, 107, 179 *See* dove image.
Blacker, Thetis 170
blessing 120
bread image 45
Buber, Martin 115
Burns, George 176-7

-C-

Canaan 4, 5, 14, 24
catastrophe (disaster) dreams 186-8
characters in dreams 159
chief baker's dream 26
chief cupbearer's dream 27
child image 164
children's dreams 48
choices, dreams help decide 28, 195
Chryostom, John 143-4
clairvoyance 1, 31, 116
clairvoyant dreams 14
classroom image 117
coat (Joseph's) image 24
Coleridge, Samuel 157
color 174-6
  amber-rose 171
  blue 156-6, 175
  green 172
  green and white 158
  pink 195
  pink and white 158
  plum 175
  rose-amber 171
  yellow 175
comfort, dreams provide 21, 98, 107, 118, 123, 183-4
conversation (dialogue) 12, 18, 35-6, 39-40, 41, 64, 84, 92, 195

converse, dreams as invitations to 18-9, 25, 41
cornerstone image 11
Corinth(ians) 97
creature images 35 *See also* animal images.
   bear with ribs in mouth 35
   Beast from the earth 102
   Beast from the sea 102
   beast with seven heads 104
   dragon 73, 74, 102, 104, 108, 129-30
   Dragon, The 102
   four creatures in Revelation 102
   leopard 35
   lion with eagle's wings 35
   monster with iron teeth 35
crying (weeping) 172-4, 184

-D-

dancing 163
Daniel 3, 23, 29-37, 71, 106, 141
David 49, 55, 56, 106
deceased loved one, dreams about 183-4
decision making, dreams affect 10-1, 158
deity 1, 2, 10, 44, 56, 61, 125
Delaney, Gayle 161
destiny 9, 26, 126
divination 43
divine prophecy 116
dove image 20
dream reporting 2
dream responses
   commitment 18, 61
   taking action 19, 72
   total experiences 18-20, 46, 97
   writing 195

dreamwork techniques,
   conversation (dialogue) 64, 195
   dramatization 195
   illustrating 195
   interviewing 196
   recording in writing with title 195
   sharing (telling, listening, discussing) 195

-E-

eagle image 70
Edison, Thomas 161
Egypt 4, 14, 21, 24, 26, 27, 28, 39-40, 43
elegant woman image 160
encouragement, dreams provide 97-8, 107, 121, 134, 135
Ezra 70-2, 100
Esther 73
everynight dreams *See* ordinary dreams.
evil woman image 154-5
extraordinary dreams 108, 169-88
Ezekiel 50

-F-

face (smiling) image 117
feminine qualities 133-4
fire image 10, 72
floating, flying, and falling 1
fragrance 135
Freud, Sigmund 191-2

Index

-G-

Gabriel 36
Gaddy, Weldon 51
Gandhi, Mahatma 161
garden(s) image 130, 134-5
gate image 131, 133
genuine dream, how to identify 51-2
geographic relocation 10, 112
Gideon 45-6
Gnuse, Robert Karl 40
goat image 20-1, 36, 159
goblet image 118
Gregory of Nazienzen 143-4
Gregory of Nyssa 143
Greek Orthodox Church 143
grief 183-4
growth 19, 33, 64, 93, 115, 117, 156, 162, 178
guidance dreams 5, 53, 56-7, 64, 112, 178, 191, 198-9

-H-

Hasidism 117
healing 5, 25, 30, 33-4, 64, 115, 124, 156, 171, 183, 196, 197
health, 33-4, 192
   mental 149
   spiritual 149
   physical 149
Hebrew letter image 117-8, 121
Holland, Chuck xi
house image 49, 86, 117, 119
Howe, Elias 161
humor 184

-I-

images 179 *See also* animal images, biblical images, *and* creature images
airplane x
apron 158
baptism 179-82
birds 179
child 164
classroom 117
color 156-8, 171, 174-6, 195
cornerstone 11
crying 172-4, 184
dancing 163
evil woman 154-5
face 118
falling 1
garden 132, 136-7
gate 131, 132
goblet 118
house 117, 154
joy 162, 164
ladder 17-9, 129, 135-6
landscape 120
light 73-4, 105, 119, 136, 142, 172
machine 175
market 118
necklace 160
orb 171
river 181
satchel 158
shade 118
shepherd 130
stars 171, 187
storm !-4R taste 174-5
tree(s) 31-2, 105, 118-21, 123, 136, 151, 163, 171, 176
watch chain 171
water 165-6, 179-80, 181-2
water pump 118
weapons 129
incubating dreams 30-1, 126

incubation 56, 133
inducing 30-1
inspiration, dreams provide 18, 64, 116, 137
instruction, dreams provide 151, 159-60
international students xi, 11
interpretation 26, 30, 32, 34, 36, 45, 50, 71, 74, 77, 85, 95, 145, 164, 178, 182, 197-8
  clever 3
  in Ancient Near East 1-3
  instantaneous (direct) 64, 72
  self 2
interpreter(s) 3, 23, 26, 27, 35, 64, 77, 146
Isaac 14, 17, 28, 39, 41, 127
Isaiah 60-1
Ismael 14
Israel 3, 39, 43, 50, 53, 74
isolation 167

-J-

Jacob x, 15, 18-21, 28, 39, 41, 50, 93, 125, 146, 194
Jeremiah 36, 51, 140
Jerome 139-40, 191
Jerusalem 29, 36, 40, 49, 98
Jesus 87-9, 92, 96, 99, 101, 104, 106, 130, 155, 172, 178
Joseph (HB) x, 2, 3, 23-8, 50, 145, 146
Joseph (NT) 83, 84
jewel image 160
Job 70
John of Patmos 101
Johnson, Robert 197
joy image 162, 164
Judah 50
Jung, Carl 19, 191-2

-K-

Kabbalah 115-6
Kelsey, Morton T. x, 34-5, 121, 192
Kushner, Harold S. 70

-L-

Laban 18, 20, 21
ladder image 17-9, 93, 131, 137-8
landscapes
  desert 172
  gray 176
laughing 173-4
light 119, 136, 142, 170, 171, 172-3
Lincoln, Abraham 194
lion image 35, 71, 102, 165
lucid dream(s) 36
Lydia 97

-M-

Macedonia(ns) 96-7
Maimonides 117
Mardochaeus 73-4
market image 118
martyrdom 129-33, 137
Mary 83-4
masculine qualities 127, 131-2
McAuliffe, Christa 186, 188
message dreams 2
Mesopotamia(ns) 4
Messiah 70, 71, 77, 82, 88, 92, 97, 106, 112, 149
Micah 51
Michael 37
Midianite 45

Index

monster image 154
Moses 39-41, 43, 56, 88, 119, 125
mysticism (Jewish) 115-8

-N-

necklace image 160
Nebuchadnezzar 3, 24, 29-34, 194, 204
Newton, John 161
nightmares 150, 156
nudity (stripped of clothing) 134

-O-

orb image 171
ordinary dreams 2, 45, 93, 141, 149-67, 189
Origen 137

-P-

Palestine 3-5, 82
parables 87
Parkinson, D. B. 161
Paul/Saul 95-9
Perpetua 129-36
Peter (Simon Peter) 91-3, 160, 179
Pharoah 3, 26-8, 40, 185, 194
Philo 117
philosophers, Jewish 117
play on words 120
pleasant dreams 149, 152, 163
Potiphar 26
prediction 2, 25, 154
    dreams of 2, 35, 36, 46, 63, 149, 185, 189

promise, God's 4,9
principles of valid interpretations 197-8
problem solving 151, 161
prophecy, divine 116
prophet(s) 39, 49-53
    false 50, 104
psychological status dreams 64

-Q-

questionable dream practices 50-1

-R-

rabbit image 176-7
ram image 36
reality 193
reassurance, dreams provide 9, 15, 21, 25, 152
recurring dreams 25, 27, 155
Reed, Henry 19, 78
rehearsal, dreams as 132
relationships 25, 152, 165
    with God promoted by dreams 5, 49, 64, 107, 141, 152, 165-7
religious experience 169
religious images 178-9
REM sleep 141, 192
repetitive dreams 25
responses to dreams 18-20, 46
revelations of deity 1, 50
river image 35, 36, 73, 181
ritual(s) 179-182
    animal sacrifice 10
rock image 29

-S-

saints 35, 102, 123-126
Samuel 40, 47-48, 125
Sanford, John 192
Sarah 14, 156
satchel image 158
Saturus 129, 133
Savary, Louis 192
Saul, King 221
Self, Bill and Carolyn 40
self-explanatory dreams 2
separation 152, 166-7
shade/shadow 118
shepherd image 88, 130
shifting scenes 102
simple message dreams 2
singing 164
Solomon 50, 55-6
song 175
source of dreams, 19, 33
Spirit, 92, 102, 140, 208
   in the 101, 102, 208
   under the power of 102
statue image 29
storm image 33-4
symbolic dreams 2, 3, 24, 25, 64, 72, 77
Synesius 137, 142-3
synchronicity 208

-T-

Talmud 115, 209
taste/tasting 174-5
telepathic dreams 188-9
telepathy 31, 116, 189
Tertullian 134, 139
throne image 35, 59, 61, 102-3, 105
transformation 33, 133, 154
transition 10-1

tree(s) image 117-9, 121, 134, 151, 171, 176
   Nebuchadnezzar's 31-2, 119
   Tree of Life 105, 116
   redwood, dancing 163

-U-

unremembered dreams 199
unpleasant dreams 149-50, 163
understanding, dreams provide 151

-V-

valid interpretation of dreams 197-8
van de Post, Laurens 19, 193
visions 5, 34-48, 50-53, 57, 63, 72, 88, 95-98, 101-9, 131, 144, 150, 183, 192, 194
visitational dreams 123-6
voice(s) 91-2, 101-3, 134, 140, 171, 172, 175

-W-

warning dreams 46, 151, 185
watch chain image 171
water image 165-6
water pump image 117
weapons image 129
Weatherhead, Leslie 33
wisdom, sources of 55
wisdom of Solomon 55
wise men's dream 85
wish fulfilling 150, 163

Index

Wordsworth, William 161
Wyeth, Nathaniel 185

-Z-

Zechariah 52
Zohar 116, 119, 124

Books for Your Personal Growth!

___Winning Your Inner Battle: Including Guided Imagery Meditations
by Jeanne Heiberg
Life is full of external dangers and problems. However, the greater battleground is with your own thoughts, feelings, and attitudes. The author, based on her personal experiences, shows you how to win the inner battle by taming your internal dragons and turning them into allies for life's journey. Each chapter ends with a guided imagery meditation that you can use yourself or in a group.
Paperbound, $8.95

___The Debris of the Encounter: A Recovery of Self
by Terre Ouwehand
During a period of psychotherapeutic exploration, Terre Ouwehand began meditating and experienced what psychologists call eidetic imagery or what mystics call inner visions. This is her story of recovery and healing. Ouwehand, a gifted playwright, works with bold images to convey an unfolding sense of a higher power at work in her life.
Paperbound, $7.95

___Whispers of The Heart: A Journey Toward Befriending Yourself
by Dale R. Olen
This book will help you magnify the voice that speaks from deep within you. The central message of this book is that all of our external behavior arises from fundamental core energies that are good. The energy to exist, the energy to act freely, and the energy to love. By learning to get in touch with these energies, you can learn to celebrate your own goodness.
Paperbound, $8.95

Order this book from your local bookstore or send in this form with your check or money order and the quantities marked above to:

Resource Publications, Inc.
160 E. Virginia St. #290
San Jose, CA 95112
(408) 286-8505

Name _____
Address _____
City _____ State____ Zip_____

Subtotal . . . . _____
*Postage and Handling . . . . _____
CA residents add 6% tax . . . . _____
TOTAL ENCLOSED . . . . _____

*Postage/Handling
$1.50 for orders under $10.00
$2.00 for orders of $10.00-$25.00
9% of order (max. $7.00) for orders over $25.00

PG